A Journey Not Chosen

By
Victoria Miller

for

All who seek a glimpse of Eternity

Copyright 2014
Victoria Miller

For
Dennis and Nicole
May you find peace

Foreword
By Dennis Miller

In February of 2004, the thirteenth fell on a Friday. Unlike the other Friday the 13th's of the previous twenty-four years, one woman was at peace. The passage of time had helped heal the wound of losing a child to miscarriage on a Friday the thirteenth. Prior such dates had accentuated the pain. That peace would last for seven more days.

Mid afternoon on the 20th, she experienced a soul draining sadness out of nowhere. It would be about an hour or so before its reason was revealed.

The nightmarish call from an emergency room doctor, told her that her son had died in a car collision. Somehow her son Jared had come to her to say goodbye prior to that call. It was a language that only the heart could understand; the mind had to wait for the words.

Vickie's journey through grief has been put into words on the following pages. Soon after Jared's passing, Vickie began experiencing dream visits from Jared and other family members. A fair amount of angst existed as to whether these dreams were simply the mind's way of coping or if they were real. The vividness and the means of communication were unlike any dreams she had ever experienced. In time, Vickie knew that these dream visits were communications from the other side.

Vickie allows the reader to understand the pain of losing a child, access to her dream visits and finally, a glimpse of dealing with the trial of the man responsible for Jared's death.

Underlying the story is a tribute to a loving and compassionate young man: our son, Jared Christopher Miller.

Table of Contents

Dream Journal

More

2004

Today my son, Jared, passed into Eternity. He had no choice and we had no advance warning. It just happened.

Jared Christopher Miller
May 1, 1981 – February 20, 2004

. . . .

Be still

And know

That I am God

Psalm 46:10

Friday, February 20th, 2004

• •

It was about 2:15 pm on Friday and I had just finished chatting with Jeanette, one of Jared's friends from high school. She was so happy, glowing with joy. Why? Because, she was expecting a baby. I had given her a baby gift and we had spent maybe twenty minutes catching up. I have always enjoyed visiting with my kids' school friends. They have all grown into mature and confident young people, ready to take on the world.

Didn't the kids just start first grade? Time just flew by once we started marking events and dates.

• •

2:20 pm

Suddenly, I am startled and overcome with sorrow. It feels like something is sucking all my energy and I am filled with a cold, heavy and endless heartache. I feel isolated, alone, dizzy and disoriented. I am in a black void where I can barely hold my head up and stand on my two feet. I need to lean on the counter as I can hardly stay alert. What is happening? This weight is unbearably heavy. It takes all of my energy to stand against this gust of wind. I am almost empty, and the only feeling that remains is sorrow. Somehow, I manage to work for about two more hours.

. . . .

It is now about 4:30. The phone rang and I answered it, "Mail Depot." The caller asks for Dennis or Vickie Miller and I respond, "This is Vickie." I had barely finished my sentence when the caller responds, "This is Doctor D-_____, at Verdugo Hills Hospital and your son Jared is dead."

I say, "Excuse ME!" I stop and I turn and rapidly walk towards Dennis and I tell him someone is saying Jared is dead. He takes the phone from my hands and listens to the caller.

Jared is dead. I sit and try to make sense of a one-sided conversation as I can only hear the words that Dennis responds with. Time has stopped. I feel like I am under some sort of trance and I am unable to respond on my own accord, controlled only by sorrow. I beg. "Please no, not my Jared." My mind is confused and my thoughts, are rambling. "What do you mean, Jared is dead?" My son is dead.

Nothing seems as it should be. The entire world feels distant and dark, with a defined barrier drawn between hot and cold or empty and full. Sorrow has overtaken my being and I am nothing.

I am thinking, No, this is not true, he can't be dead. Jared has to finish college. He wants to go on a mission trip to the Congo in Africa. He wants a wife and children. He wants to play music in a Christian rock band. He wants to build a youth camp. He wants to get a masters' degree, and yet at age twenty two, my son is dead.

I remember going home, washing my face and putting on a nightgown. Dennis was making a few phone calls. He was again talking to the hospital. It was too late to donate major organs, but it was still possible to harvest heart valves, tissues, and ligaments. We had never discussed with Jared what his wishes might have been in this situation, but knowing him, we believe he would have chosen to help others if he could.

Dennis and I went to bed. I know I did not sleep. My eyes are wide open, almost glued-open. My thoughts are confused and jumbled up. I am just laying here waiting, listening to the clock tick and the furnace, go on and off, trying to find peace, trying to settle my thoughts.

It would be days before I saw sleep again.

The Day After

. . . .

Why does living have to be so complicated? I just need
to pick my head up off the pillow, swing my legs
towards the floor, set my feet down and use what little
strength I have and take a step, then another. The
bathroom is not too far away. Please, some warm water
to soothe my skin. Why is it so hard to move, both
mentally and physically? I am drained. I have no desire
to move forward, to eat, or to sleep.

. . . .

We need to make arrangements with the mortuary. We
need to order flowers. The flowers need to be pure
white roses and evergreen swags. Jared is a gentle, soft,
and old wise soul. White will display his pure heart.
Next we need to write an article for the newspaper, make
arrangements for work, buy Dennis a suit, decide on,
what dress I would wear, talk with the investigating
police in California and talk with the local pastor about
the service. People arriving, people talking, flowers at
the door, food on the table and in the refrigerator and yet
I have no interest in a bite. Please, time needs to stop!!!!

. . . .

"Jared, are you all right? What is heaven like? I love you! I miss you! Please come back to us."

. . . .

. Jared's friends will pack up his things and drive his white truck home from California. Twenty plus friends from college will be arriving in a few days, driving from Fullerton as well as Hope University staff and camp staff. Local friends will house most of the travelers, making sure they are fed and taken care of, getting them to and from the church and our home.

Dennis and I picked out a simple pine coffin and selected a burial site at Belcrest Memorial Park. Someday we too will rest next to our son, on a slight slope just a few yards from my mom and dad.

Tuesday

· · · · · · · · · · · · · · · · · · ·

Jared will be coming home today. He will not sneak in
the side door through the laundry room and attempt to
scare me. He will not say his famous, "Waz up?" He
will not give me a hug and say "I love you Mom". He
will not tell me that I am shorter than him and that he
can see the gray hair on the top of my head.

Today, Jared will be flown home with the help of others.
We have been advised not to meet the plane at the
Portland Airport. Wait and let the mortuary staff, handle
all the details. My younger brother Clark lives in the
Portland area and he will meet the plane. He'll watch as
the airline and the mortuary personnel greet each other
and make the exchange. Then he will follow Jared
home. I now know it is for the best that we did not go.
Just one more sad memory to play over and over in our
minds as time continues here on earth.

So we wait. Home seems to be the right place to be.

Suddenly it is like a monsoon outside. The sky is
weeping with tears and the thunder booms in the
distance. As the plane approaches the airport, the sky
will not settle. It is not until about the time the van

17

arrives in Salem that calm returns to the heavens. Standing on my front porch, are Dennis and I, our daughter Nicole and her fiancé Greg. We are all amazed at just how angry the sky is. Maybe God is letting it be known that it was too soon for Jared to return to heaven. Jared is home.

Someday, maybe, I will have the courage and strength to ask my brother about his experience at the airport and the drive to our hometown. Clark told me once or twice that he looked up to my son, his nephew. He sensed his wisdom and strength and wished to be close to the joy and wonder that surrounded him.

. . . .

For the last two or three days I have noticed that there is this dumb black cat outside in the yard. It follows me around the house. I am inside and it is outside. If I move, it moves to the next window in that room. It has such a sad meow and it will not stop. This goes on for a few days. Even Dennis, recognizes that it is following me around the house. We finally scare it away.

Wednesday

. . . .

Today we get to see Jared. He is waiting for us to arrive at the mortuary.

During the drive to South Salem, I was anxious and scared not knowing how I would respond to seeing Jared. I am unsure of my emotions, but I had to come. Upon our arrival we entered the front door. To our surprise, two friends, Ed and John, were in the lobby. They had come to say good bye themselves. Not long ago Ed, too, lost a son. He knew what our thoughts were.

John stopped me and wished to share a story, one I will always cherish. He said that last Christmas, which was about two months ago, he had been at our place of business. Jared had stopped by on his way back to Fullerton where he attended College at Hope University. He watched me, Jared and Dennis as we said our goodbyes and hugged for a few moments. He said that in watching our private moment, he saw our special bond and the depth of love that we shared for each other.

I look up and I see the small name tag on the wall. I hesitate for but a moment, thinking, "Will I survive this day and will I ever be the same again?" I walk in and there is Jared. He is home.

I stop for a moment. I am afraid to take a step forward. My mind is thinking I do not want to remember him cold and lifeless as he lay at this moment. I wondered if I should reach forward and touch him? Would a kiss from his mom wake him up? This can't be real, but I know it is.

Friday
A gathering of friends

. . . .

Tonight some of Jared's friends will come to visit. I need to get the house cleaned up and order an assortment of pizzas. This is about all I can do for today.

As Jared's friends begin to arrive, the door is constantly being knocked on. It reminds me of when the kids were in high school.

. . . .

During Jared's senior year he was highly involved with the drama program at McNary High School. His advisor, Linda Baker was an exceptional teacher who encouraged her students with strong and gentle guidance. That year Jared had the opportunity to be the stage manager and the set and scene designer for the Will Rogers Follies. He excelled in both areas.

I remember the day of the opening night. I went to the school looking for Jared. I was told that he and the cast were in the Little Theatre. When I found him, he was

21

giving a pep talk to his classmates. I had never seen him in a capacity quite like this before. I watched his fellow youth intently looking up to him with respect and confidence. They admired his authority and leadership. I was in awe.

(I smile for a moment because I remember.)

. . . .

The door bell continues to ring and college friends come and go and return again. The evening brought many silly and heart-warming stories. Friends told secrets and stories that only they knew. My little boy, now a man, was friends with many.

Saturday
The Funeral
Please give me strength

. . . .

We need to arrive at the Church a couple of hours early.
Pastor Tim will be arriving ahead of time with Jenna,
Jared's friend and companion. She was with him when
he died. We had heard about her many times from Jared
and yet, we had not met before. She just wanted to talk
for a bit before the service.

Both Dennis' and my siblings began to arrive. They
were ushered into the private room with us. Once, for a
moment, I snuck out for a sip of water and I glimpsed all
the people entering. I wondered if I should greet the
visitors, not comprehending who or how many there
were.

When the time came, we were led down the hallway to
the sanctuary. The pews were full and guests were
standing in every corner. It was then that I understood
when the mortuary had said, "that they could not contain
the situation." There must have been at least three or
four hundred people. I could not even begin to tell you

who was there as only a few faces registered in my thoughts. The service continued for almost two hours. Most of us hope for a few friends to remember us, but I was in awe. All these people came to support us and to say good-bye to Jared.

Suddenly I think, "Wait, how is Jared getting here?" He would not walk in the door and smile. He would not skate in on his roller blades. He was to come in a pine box. As I sat there, I kept looking around waiting for one of those miracles people talk about. I looked high and low expecting to see Jared sitting up on the ledge or the upper railing waving at me, letting me know he was there. "This has to be a mistake!" I beg, "Jared, please walk through the door and surprise us. We will forgive you for teasing us. Please, Jared, I miss you."

The day before

. . . .

Jared called to say that he would be at Angeles Crest Christian Camp for most of the weekend. He was checking in and promised to call when he got home Sunday night. There were many youth coming for Winter Camp.

. . . .

Jared was attending Hope University in Fullerton and was close to getting his Bachelor's Degree in Youth Ministry. If my memory serves me right, he had just one term left before graduating from college. He was excited because he was offered the Program Director job for two years at ACCC. It was not his original plan, but this plan was just as good, if not even better. He had hoped to someday return to the Northwest and become the Director at Camp Arrah Wanna.

Before he accepted the job offer at ACCC he called Dennis and I to see if we were okay with him not returning home as planned. (How do you respond when you see your child happy and enriching the lives of the youth who crossed his path?) We were happy for him and this great opportunity and yet a bit sad because we would not see him every week like we had hoped for.

Many days later

. . . .

I recall moments in time and I wondered, "Did I somehow know in the back of my mind that this day would come, or was I just too much of a worry wart?

As I had laid in the hospital on May 1, 1981, a few hours after having a c-section, I was so cold. Warmed blankets and pain killers did nothing for me. I was still half numb from a spinal, and yet riddled with pain and frozen cold. Was this the beginning of my fear?

A few years before Jared's passing, Dennis and I had met up with him and our daughter Nicole in the Sacramento area. Nicole was arriving back from a Nature Conservancy job in the southeast, heading to Sequoia National Park. We all made plans to be tourists, to hike and play for a few days.

Nicole was the first to depart, anxious to start her new position in the park. Dennis, Jared and I had time to get lunch before he headed back to college, his summer job and internship at ACCC, Angeles Crest Christian Camp. As we parted, I had this overwhelming sense that someday Jared would die in a car wreck. I was consumed with fear. It almost felt like I knew of his death before it was to actually happen. As we drove home I hardly closed my eyes, I even developed a slight hand tremor and tension was my companion as we drove. At that time we did not have a cell phone so I had no way to contact him. Even if I could I probably would not have told him about my feelings, as I would not have wanted to make him nervous. After everyone arrived at their destinations I was finally able to relax. I knew I had some future knowledge, though I had no idea of when or where, only that one day my fears would become a nightmare come true.

Analyzing the wind of sorrow

* *

Over and over I have analyzed what happened the day my son died at 2:20 pm. It was almost two hours after he had died before we got the phone call. Yet the time listed on his death certificate was 2:20.

How could I have known, and yet had not known?

Dennis and I believe that love transcends space and time and that when Jared died, he came to tell me so and to say goodbye. He came to me from hundreds of miles away at the moment of his death.

I believe that when we die it is but a second, or a moment, or a blink that our soul, the essence of who we are, is still alive. Our physical bodies that we know may be lifeless, but we walk out of our bodies, the same person that we were a moment ago; that our soul, our energy, has the ability to take on a new form-maybe like a solid shadow which is the same image of ourselves. We have evolved, much like the process that the caterpillar has when it becomes the butterfly.

I really do not believe that I can describe it correctly, but

Jared is still Jared and Jared is still my son. In the awake state, I could not see him, but he was there, telling me he had to go. Maybe someday my subconscious will allow me to see what happened and allow me to make sense of what I felt and sensed.

Friday, February 20, 2004
The day of no return

. . . .

It was around noon. Jared had picked up his friend
Jenna. She is a fellow student and friend from Oregon.
He had arranged weekend employment for her to help
with the youth winter camp. They picked up lunch and
headed up the mountain road outside of La Crescenta
towards Angeles Crest Christian Camp, located just
outside of La Canada. It was a familiar drive. Jared had
spent many days and hours working at the camp.

It is a two lane highway. Jared was approaching a curve
with a blind corner. He was a good driver, following the
rules of the road. He did not know what was waiting for
him as he approached the curve and rounded the corner.
My hope is that he never felt that instance of panic or
fear.

As Jared was proceeding up the mountain and into the
curve, a government truck was coming down. It was
being driven by an employee of the Forest Service who
had crossed the double lines and was driving in Jared's
lane. Jared had no time to react and nowhere to go.

The other driver basically ran over the top of the Jared's side of the car. Most of Jared's vital organs were damaged beyond repair and he was not considered viable to transport via airlift.

From what we have been told, the highway was closed for hours. Accident reconstruction crews, investigating police, emergency crews and fire department personnel were on site, collecting the evidence late into the evening.

One day I was told

One day I was told
A story of old, a story that reaches across time,
A tale of He, who carries our sorrow.

One day, as he was shaving,
His beard, now centuries old
The blade he held, it drew blood.

He was bleeding, His heart was breaking,
His essence, his core,
Heavy, overflowing with endless sorrow.

Today, I was told
His being could hold the agonies of all eternity.

Close your eyes, imagine, wonder, take a peek
Over there, through the soft mist,
The fog shimmering with dew,
Slightly transparent,

And if you squinted, you might get a glimpse,
Of He who held our journey
He stood, tears falling,
Placing, all within his heart.

Vickie Miller

2012

It is my hope that you will discover wonder and joy as you journey with me through confusion and sadness, as I dream walk with Jared and other members of my family. May you also find evidence of our awesome Creator so that you too may use the phrase, "to bear witness to His Glory." For me, faith has become knowledge and my dream visits a source of strength and hope.

I do not remember the exact date that these visits began, just that it was within the first few weeks of Jared's passing. A couple of years ago I had my first experience with such happenings, when my father arrived in the dream world to inform me that he was looking out for my son, the child I miscarried in 1978 on Friday the thirteenth. At that time I had no clue that someday in the future my dad might arrive again to tell me yet again that he was looking out for another son, Jared.

These experiences are as real as any event in my life. They are not always easy to understand as the communication I receive is at a faster rate. I do not always hear the words, but they are placed in my mind. What I do understand is more complete and clear. I have a better understanding and clarity of the word or sentence expressed more like I can feel and sense its meaning. Each night as I settle in for the evening and begin to prepare for sleep, I plead for yet another visit. One thing that I have learned is that I cannot control when they will happen, but I know that they will. I am not always sure if I am there or that they are here, but for a time or two we are together.

My dream visits are proof of Eternity and what lies beyond our lives here on earth. Many of my family members have reached across the barrier between this life and Eternity. Some I have known here and others from generations past. As you read about my dream visits, you will discover that the baby I miscarried in 1978 grew up in Heaven and that he is a twin. At the time of my miscarriage the doctor did not inform me that my one baby was really two.

My twins radiate pure love and energy. Matt has a silly sense of humor much like Jared and their father Dennis. He is a strong leader. Michael is more reserved and quiet, content with standing back, watching his brothers, patient and calm. I so often think of the words, "I can only imagine" and yet I know.

I would rather have a mind,

opened,

by wonder,

than

one closed by belief

Gerry Spence

Dream Journal

Through the eyes of my Mama
(Jared's title for these writings)

2004

I awoke stunned, eyes wide open, not sure what just happened, only that I knew that I had just seen Jared and I heard him talk. Yet, I knew he lay lifeless in a wooden pine box.

The last time I had seen him was the Wednesday after he died, cold and silent, with his favorite childhood toy, Bon Bon, the ragged blue bunny, now tucked under his arm.

Jared and the blueprints
2004

. . . .

I am standing in what seems to be a middle school office
leaning over the front counter. A male teacher asks me
to go to his classroom to get something from his desk. I
head in that direction thinking to myself, "Maybe I work
here."

As I walk into the classroom, I notice two teen-age girls
rummaging through the teacher's desk. My impression
is that they are searching for money.

I start to walk towards them. I hope to shoo them off
before they commit a crime. My actions cause them to
run and I begin to chase them. Suddenly I stop. I am
centered within a door frame.

I am frozen, and an invisible barrier holds me in place. I
stand there. Before me walks Jared and two other young
men who seem to be about the same age, early twenties I
would guess. They seem unaware of my presence. I feel
like I am looking inside a slightly rustic & dirty window.

I stand stunned, wondering, thinking, just watching.
They are unrolling blueprints, holding them up and
scoping out the project they plan to build. I do not know
what they are intending to build, just that it is an
awesome idea. I cannot make out the words. I only

know that I can hear Jared's voice.

I am startled and I wake up instantly, almost shocked awake. I realize that I just heard and saw my son who recently died and woke up in heaven. I knew whatever his task was that it was laid out in these blueprints handed to him from God.

God
has planted eternity
in the human heart.

Ecclesiastes 3:11

Jared and his brother - 2004

. . . .

I find myself entering a warehouse. Dennis is living in
the upstairs loft. In my dream state Dennis and I are
separated which is not the situation in the awake state. I
am going to tell him that our marriage is eternal and I
want to resume our life together.

I start to climb the stairs, and I realize that I am taking
steps that are all shapes, widths, heights and lengths. It
is quite strenuous work to climb up on these steps and
my legs are tiring quickly. I can actually feel the burn as
I stretch towards the top.

I notice that Dennis is sleeping in his bed and I become
aware of another presence with him. I am ready to
panic, thinking I am too late to reconcile, but then I
notice, that it is Jared! He is comforting his dad. I can
sense his strength and stability surrounding Dennis, as
Dennis is trying to recover from the loss of our child.

As I stand relieved, my breathing relaxes and the visit
changes from one location to another. I suddenly find
myself somewhere else, in the most brilliant white
serene place I have ever been. It is purity. It is
freshness. It is clarity in a solid form. I am sitting on a
boulder. It is perfectly situated at the just the right
height for my comfort.

Slowly walking towards me are a young boy and a young man. The boy seems to be about nine or ten and the young man in his early twenties. They stop about three feet away, directly in front of me. The young boy and I are seriously looking at each other. I am trying to figure out if I know him or not. Both of us tilt our heads almost in unison, mirroring each other with slight movements, looking, kind of like when you are checking someone out. This continues for five to ten seconds. I find myself asking a question yet I am making a statement.

"You are my son! Aren't you?" I do not know how I know this, but I do.

He stands up straight and looks me in the eyes and ever so proudly he answers, "Yes! I am." He lets it be known that he has waited a long time to meet me and he is proud that I am his mother.

I am quite startled that I wake up, not because of any fear, but because I had just met my child that I had miscarried. He thrived and grew up in heaven! He is proud of me, his mom!

• •

(At this time in my life I had not yet realized that the two boys were twins. I was never told that I had miscarried twins, so I just assumed they were the same person and I

was viewing two different stages of his life. He carries such peace, contentment, joy, serenity, calmness and love. He is my son.

If we could see
the miracle
of a single flower clearly,
our
whole life would change

Buddha

My eyes are the same -September 15, 2004

. . . .

Things feel slightly foggy, sort of out of focus. This is the first time I really experience someone placing a thought in my head. It is precise and clear and in no way do I feel violated.

Jared is telling me, "Mom! I am in the car that is approaching. My eyes are the same, but I am a little different."

I am standing in the street in front of our house and I see a car approaching. It slows down as it gets close and turns into the driveway in front of me. Jared parks the car on the left side which is where I typically park. He opens the door and steps out. I continue to stand in the street, since I am awestruck and I do not quite know how to react. Jared's backside is facing me. He then turns west and is facing the driver side of the car. He is dressed in royal blue clothing. I believe it is some special rock climbing clothing. He has on a waist belt with attachments, like a small hammer-pick, and various carabiners. He is holding a water bottle and he starts to drink from it. As he is tilting back to swallow, I wonder if it is a Nalgene bottle, his favorite brand. I begin to take a step forward and I wake up. As I wake up I am thinking about Lamborghini and Delorean cars. I did not take note of what type of car Jared drove, but during Jared's teen years he made it known that he really would like one of these cars.

Jared totally seemed the same, and I believe I could smell his scent. For just a moment, in the half-awake state, I heard someone say "Mom." I never did see what was different about him as he had said.

. . . .

A few moments later, I woke Dennis to tell him about Jared and the visit. When I finished telling him about the visit, he commented how he was just talking to him, not even sure Jared would hear him, hoping that he was listening, saying, "that now would be a good time to come visit your mom, she really needs you."

. . . .

Be like the bird,
pausing, in his flight
on limb too slight,
feels it give way,
yet sings,
knowing he has wings

Victor Hugo

Dad

My father is going to take me to see Jared

. . . .

I am pulling into the parking lot at work. Something seems odd, and it takes but a second to realize that the Espresso Cart is gone. In its place are some broken concrete blocks. I navigate through the blocks and park the car.

I wonder "What happened to the coffee cart? It was there yesterday. Our tenants never mentioned that they were moving." I think, oh well.

I open the door of my car and get out. As I turn and walk towards the building I now notice that there is snow on the ground. "What the heck? Where did that come from?" I decide to walk through the parking lot instead of my usual routine behind the building and through the back door. As I walk forward, I see someone sitting on the handicapped ramp in the snow. She is putting stamps on her padded envelopes. I sit and help and we talk for a bit. It is my friend Brenda. A few seconds later a car pulls up on my right side.

A few years ago you could actually do that, but today that would be impossible as the structure of the road has

48

changed.

I yell across to the driver and say, "You can't park there. It is a sidewalk." (I realize that I am in a dream and I can distinguish the dream from reality.)

I turn back towards Brenda and I start to stand up. Now I see my dad. He died in 1979. It has been so long since I have seen him! He is vibrant, healthy, and standing right in front of me. We grab each other and hold tightly onto each other's upper arms. Surprised and happy I say, "Dad, where have you been?"

I knew that he has been in heaven, but it's my dad and need to ask the silly human question. I am a bit surprised only because he appears younger than I remember him. He still has a receding hairline and he clearly is my father. He says something to me but I do not understand the words nor do I hear them out loud. They have been placed, again, in my mind.

I ask him, "Have you seen Jared? Do you know where Jared is?"

My eyes follow him as he turns in the direction of my car.

The snow is gone and I see a group of younger people. I get a sense that they are about college age. My father impresses upon me that Jared is over with them. He is the one with the dog and that he will take me to him.

This group of people is patiently waiting. There is a traveling carnival in the vacant lot behind my building. I know that they are waiting for the carnival to open as they want to attend and play the silly games. A few of them have balloons. I notice them flowing with the breeze.

I see the dog that my Dad mentioned. This group of people, have become kind of compacted. I assume that Jared is in the middle of the huddle as he is not in the outer ring.

I am thinking, "How odd, that Jared would be the one with the dog." Here on earth Jared was somewhat nervous around dogs.

I take one step with my Dad. I cannot center myself in the visit and I wake up.

Days later my upper arms still ache, like they were bruised. So much for assuming the physical strength of a soul, my Dad would be gentle. His heavenly body holds a force just like our human bodies.

I go to nature,
to be soothed and healed,
and to have my senses,
put in tune once more.

John Burroughs

Birthday Dream Card
December 23, 2004

• • • • • • • • • • • • • • • • • • •

Today is my birthday. It is the first birthday since losing
my son. It is the first birthday I would just like to forget.
Trying to stay focused on life is not easy. I try to
remember that without me, the Jared we all know and
love would not be. Jared did not forget what today was.

Today I received a mental version of a birthday card. It
was a great way to start my day. I saw the birthday card
in the dream world.

The card was simple and yet intriguing. I was pretty
sure it was from Jared though he did not sign his name.
Everything about it was just like what Jared would do.

The upper left hand corner had a capital, "I" with a hand
drawn heart next to it. Located in the middle, just a bit
off center towards the left, was a hand-drawn picture of a
flower, like a daisy. Off to the side of the flower was the
word, "mommy." The lower right corner had the
number thirty-five, drawn in numerical figures. It
appeared like 3:5.

At first I was a bit confused about the thirty-five. It was

not how old I was. It was placed in the lower right corner just like you would sign a card.

A few days later I figured out what the thirty-five meant. You know those name cards that are made, similar in size to a baseball card. You usually find them at a Christian bookstore. The cards have a person's name and the bible verse related to them. Well, Jared's name is linked to Proverb's 3:5.

Trust in the Lord with all your heart,

lean not on your own understanding,

In all your ways acknowledge Him,

And

He will make your paths straight

Proverbs 3:5 – 3:6

Jesus and various ancestors

. . . .

I find myself in a low-lit room, standing in front of a sofa, with chairs on each side. Dennis is seated in the chair to the right. He looks like he is wondering, where are we? Even with the dim lights, I can still distinguish that two other people are seated nearby, one on the sofa and one in the other chair. It takes just a second for me to realize that it is Jared and his brother. My other son is trying to talk to me, yet I do not understand. Again, I feel like the thoughts are being placed in my mind. I look at Dennis and see that he is confused, trying to understand who I am talking to.

Five or six more people appear on the sofa, one after the other, maybe five seconds apart. As they appear, they all sit in the middle of the sofa. One person tells me, "you should not have given up on your genealogy search so soon." I get the impression that these people are ancestors of mine, waiting to reveal themselves to me. I can only remember a couple of names, Jungworth or Jingworth, and Olson. They are placing thoughts into my head. I am aware of them, but I cannot understand and I cannot keep up with what they are saying. It's more like they are introducing themselves to me. So far there are four or five men who have sat down, then a woman appears. She too sits in the middle and she looks to be about thirty years of age.

I ask her, 'Who are you?" She says, "I am Grandma Minnie." She is my mother's mom.

Someone is standing in front of me. I am now on my knees, wondering, how did I get down on the floor? I reach towards the person and He reaches for me. We touch for only a second, though long enough for me to realize it is "He" who holds my saddened soul together. I do not see His face, but I do feel the brush of His clothing. My eyes and mind are wide open. It is awesome to realize that in all of eternity he had time to be with me.

As I try to comprehend the fact that He knew me and He had time for me, my thoughts marvel at the concept of just Him and me for a moment or two.

I look up and see that He is now behind the sofa about twenty feet away. He is carrying my daughter Nicole. Her body radiates love and purity. She is my beautiful daughter. I realize that I do not need to worry about her anymore because she is protected by Him. He says, "She is mine and I shall carry her."

 Have you realized who I speak of? Jesus, God our Creator.

My soul, my essence,
is carved like a rock,
I realize I am child of God.
As I look to the heavens,
I dream to be one,
with him,
I long to soar
between the
heavens and the earth.

Vickie Miller

My Name is Matt and tell daddy...

· ·

This visit starts like a regular dream. I am with a friend. We are driving and searching for higher ground in the Seattle area. Flood waters are rising and we need to find a safe place.

We find our way to a friend of the friend's house. I am fooling around with an old camera. I point it towards a lighted wall and look through the viewfinder. As I am thinking about taking a picture, I see Jared in the viewfinder. He looks about ten years old and is just smiling at me. I begin to wonder what kind of dream this is when I realize it is a visit. Off to Jared's side is his brother. He looks to be about the age he would be if my body had, not miscarried him. Since meeting him for the first time I have been trying to name him. What name would seem right?

· · · · · · · · · · · · · · · · · · ·

Two days before this visit as I was driving home I was doing my normal talking into space wondering if anyone was listening. I was talking out loud. "Surely someone in heaven would have named you" (referring to my first child) and I wondered what it was. I guess I should stop

57

trying to come up with a name as I am sure it had been done many years before.

. . . .

My son begins to speak and I clearly understand, "My name is Matt and tell Daddy that I love photography, just like him." Matt is standing there holding a boxy antique camera and smiling.

Your life is like a tapestry,
being woven by God and history,
on an enchanted loom,
every bobble of the shuttle,
has meaning,
every thread is important.

Richard Nelson

Jared says, "We are all of the Kingdom of God"

· · · · · · · · · · · · · · · · · · · ·

It is always interesting how sometimes my dreams appear to be just a plain dream and then they turn into something more.

My mom and I are held hostage at a humanitarian conference. Many attempts at solving critical issues have been discussed and debated. We have been separated from each other and now someone comes to get me and to take me to her. She is sick and lying on a table or bed. She is dying. I seem to know that she has had a heart attack. No one told me, I just knew. The people who are trying to help her, say, that she is talking to someone, yet they see no one in the room. I notice some weird bubbles on her forehead, and I tell her that I love her.

I look up and in the upper left corner of the ceiling I see Jared's face peeking through. I sense that Matt is with him as well. Jared has an infectious smile that he always had here in the earthly plane. I can feel his happiness. He says many things that I do not understand. He is talking too fast for me to comprehend his words. Finally

I pick up on one sentence. **"We are all of the Kingdom of God."**

. . . .

It does not matter what religious group you belong to. Not "one" has it more right than any of the others.

. . . .

We know the truth,

not only by reason,

but by the heart

Blaise Pascal

April 26th, 2006
Jared says, "Matt is really cool"

• •

Jared and I are in a room and he is sitting on a sofa. I
am standing in front of him with probably six feet of
space between us. I know we are talking and I feel like I
have asked many questions. I begin to think that this is
just a regular dream, but suddenly I know that Jared
knows my thoughts and he smiles and I know it is more.
I know that he is using his abilities to keep me calm,
helping me stay in the moment. He starts a sentence
with "In my neighborhood," implying heaven, but I lose
the rest of the sentence. Then he clearly says, "Matt is
really cool."

I see two family members in the background who
believe strongly in reincarnation.

Jared instills knowledge or a thought about telling them
that there is no reincarnation. It is not true. We are who
we are, unique individuals each made in the image of
God. As I turn, I attempt to hush the family members as
their commotion is distracting me. I wake up.

Upon waking from this visit I feel like every nerve in my body is alive and tingling. This is a very good sensation.

Happiness is reflective,
Like
the light of heaven

Washington Irving

May 3, 2006
Grandma Minnie named Matt

• •

I find that I am on a slow moving parade float. I am trying to attach Jared's clarinet to a camera tripod. I know it sounds dumb, but most dreams visits tend to start a little odd. Mixing the two worlds is not always easy. I am riding with a group of people that either personally know Jared or know of Jared. I am unsure of what the occasion is, but it appears to be a happy one.

Most of the participants are facing towards me, and among the group is Jared. He stands about five feet from me. I see that my dad is towards the back of the float. I also notice my Uncle Leo walking alongside the float. I notice his smile and then I see Matt. He is walking along, wearing a letterman's jacket.

Jared tells me that, I'll be all right, meaning me and my sorrow. As always the conversation continues but most is lost as I wake up. Neither, my Dad or Uncle Leo say anything. They are just there and very happy. I do notice Leo's huge smile and his wavy brown hair.

I sense that Jared is sad, but only because I am sad. Otherwise he overflows with happiness.

Jared clearly has a message and he says, "Grandma Minnie named Matthew. Sometimes they call him Matt, and sometimes they call him Mike for short. He is also named after someone called Michael Doss or Cross."

If God did not exist,

It would be necessary

to invent him

Francois Voltaire

October 15, 2006
"Mom, I want you to build my camp"
A command of sorts

· ·

Today I am walking in a beautiful garden with my Uncle
Leo. Greenery and flowers line the walking paths. We
walk for about five minutes or so and then my Aunt
Susie appears. We walk towards a set of double doors.
They open into what seems to be a fancy hotel and we
walk into the beautiful lobby.

I look up and there is my dad. Standing next to him is a
young boy about ten years old. I ask my dad if this is
his brother, Sebastian. My dad, says to me, "No, he is
your other son."

Again, I have confirmation of another son. I am still
confused, but it is becoming, more clear that I may have
twins.

Somehow I am now sitting in a chair in a half circle with
other people. I am on the end and it seems that I know

the people seated next to me. Someone is hidden behind them, and I notice a third person. I am thinking that I know the shape of those legs and they are familiar. I lean forward and as I do, the other person does too. It is Jared, fully grown, yet he looks a bit younger then he really was. We reach across those seated between us and tightly hug each other.

With his arms around me, Jared says, "Mom, I love you". I can actually feel his love. It radiates from his soul.

With a command and a determined voice, he says, "MOM, I want you to build my camp." As I acknowledge his desire, he is pleased, that I understand his message, and pleased that I wish to make his dream come true.

The winds of grace
blow all the time.
All we need to do
is set our sails.

Ramakrishna

May 21, 2007
Jared and the patting hug

. . . .

What the heck? My mom and I are driving in her old
Lincoln, the same one she and dad had when I was a kid.
She is the one driving which is odd since her hands are
pretty much useless as Arthritis and Parkinson's have
taken her mobility away. I take notice that she is using
her fingertips to steer the car which again seems odd.
She turns the car and heads down a steep slope. I am
thinking I'll never be able to back this car up and out.
There is no place to turn around at the bottom either.
Once we arrive at the bottom, she jumps out of the car,
leaving me somewhat confused. She dives into a creek
bed which only has a couple of inches of water. She
dives under the rocks. Again I am confused.

Suddenly I find myself in a room with my Aunt Susie
and Aunt Mary. As I write these words, they have both
been in heaven for some time. We are attending a
luncheon in this beautifully decorated room. I realize

72

that the luncheon is for my mom, an after the funeral gathering.

I see my mom laying in a casket. She sits up, beautiful and much younger than this morning, with dark brown hair, seeming to be about 40 years old and overflowing with happiness.

Susie and Mary both indicate that my Dad is in an adjoining room, so I decide to go look for him. As I enter that room it feels like a gymnasium, filled with an assortment of people. As I stand in the room, I am turning around in a circle viewing people and watching the happenings, searching for my Dad. After turning around maybe three times, I see Jared and I stop. We begin to walk towards each other and as we get close, we hug. This hug is a real hug, yet it feels odd. I do not feel a material or physical body, but a body of energy, still totally my son Jared. What I feel is solid energy, full of love, warmth and strength. Jared is also patting me on the back. As we continue hugging, each of our hands pat the other in unison. We talk some, but most is lost as I wake up.

I ask him, "Where is your brother?" and He replies, "He is off doing some important work in Heaven." He also tells me that he was at Nicole and Greg's wedding, playing and chasing the little kids around.

I asked him a direct question pertaining to Christ, "Would Jesus return to earth in my lifetime?" He said,

"Yes."

My intention in asking the question was in reference to the second coming of Christ. He did not say when, just that it would happen in my lifetime on earth.

As this visit was ending and I began to wake up, I see Jared wearing the cross necklace that Dennis and I had given him.

The heavens declare,

the glory of God

Psalm 19:1

Matt's name
May 22, 2007

. . . .

I have this feeling of being in a cave. The lighting seems very low, like in early morning or early evening as the sun has just come up or gone down. Along with a few other people I am sitting in a circle, like sitting around a campfire, yet there is no fire. I sense that all the people here are family members, but I cannot make out their faces. Jared and Matt are here, and they are dressed in black leather clothing sort of like a motorcyclist might wear. I sense that Uncle Frank and his wife, Vi, are also here.

Someone in the circle thinks it's cute and funny that Aunt Clara likes to refer to herself as the family matriarch. They also acknowledge that Clara and I share an interest in genealogy and they are pleased.

Jared says to stop worrying about Nicole because she will be fine.

I turn to who I believe is Matt and I ask him, "So, what is your name?

He sat there teasing me, tilting his head back and forth, kind of like when one juggles a ball back and forth between your hands, "Matt or Michael, Michael or Matt, Matt or Michael." He looks directly into my eyes and says," So which one, do you like?"

I respond with, "Dad and I kind of like Matt for your name."

He resumed his teasing and just left it up in the air. One thing I do know: he is Jared's older brother. I may be confused as to how many sons, and their names, but the fact is, I did lose a baby by miscarriage in 1978.

As I begin to wake up I sense one more thing. Both Jared and Matt have a young lady sitting next to them, and I get a real sense that they are their girlfriends. There is also someone else just behind them.

Life is not measured

by

the breaths we take,

but by the moments

that take

our breath away

unknown

A Promise to God
May 2007

. . . .

Each new visit makes it increasingly clear that these are more than typical dreams. These visits remain in my memory as real happenings, as real as any moment in time. A typical dream is almost always lost or forgotten when I wake up.

This particular visit has adjusted the direction of what I thought my life was going to be. Not knowing what my life would ever really be, I now know that it is hoped that I will fulfill my son's dream of building a youth retreat or a youth camp.

. . . .

I find myself driving down a road, noticing that up ahead I will need to make a choice as to what direction to turn. I am approaching a fork and I need to decide to go left or right. Keeping to the main road will only keep me driving straight like going north and south along the freeway. I decide or I find myself veering off to the right to see what is over there.

It appears to be early evening as I now find myself sitting with three or four men in a low-lit area, outdoors. They all seem to be familiar. Do I know them? Yes, but who are they?

A conversation has started and it seems to go on for quite some time. I remember saying and thinking that I will write all this stuff down because it is important. When I wake up I want to remember all that was said. I know that I am in the dream world and I need to remain calm in order to hold myself there longer, otherwise I will wake up before I want to. I wrote many things down yet the only written thing that remained was something about 11 / 9, November 9th. Something was going to happen around or on that date but I am uncertain as to what.

One of the men said to me that it was my time to come to heaven, and I said, "Cool, I am ready."

Oh, how I wished to be with my sons. The same man also said that I had passed all the tests. I took one step and stopped.

I am not sure what made me stop, but I found myself saying, "Wait, I cannot go." Instantly I am on my knees and I am promising God that I will build Jared's Camp.

Was I just in the presence of God? How did I not know it? Did I just make a promise to our Creator? Why

would He think that I was capable of such a task?
Really, me! I have no such experience or training.

It is not quite the same as when you make a promise to friends, acquaintances, or family. To make a promise, to do something in the actual presence of God--well, it consumes my core.

One of the men said one more thing. He said that Nicole and Greg would be adopting a baby. Wait, did he say twins or did he say a baby? It would all be very last minute, not planned by the birth mother.

. . . .

Update: November 9, 2009

My daughter Nicole and her husband Greg received a phone call today. They had been waiting to adopt. They had been chosen once before but the birth mother had changed her mind.

Today, almost at the last minute, a young girl made the choice to give her baby up for adoption and she was due any day. The birth mother was interested in them. Within an hour or two, they decided to head to Idaho to meet the birth mother, hoping that when she put a face to the pictures on the web, she would like them and choose them. By evening the next day, she had chosen them as the parents of her baby. Any moment now we were going to be grandparents. We fell in love with "little miss bug a boo" even before she arrived. A few days later little Miss Anala was born.

So she was not born on November 9, but she became a member of our family that day.

Never
be afraid
to sit awhile
and think.

Lorraine Hansberry

June 11, 2007
Introductions

. . . .

Ever since I was a little girl I can always remember
Cindy. She is about 1 ½ years younger than me. In the
beginning my parents and the doctors were sure she was
just like any other child. Little did anyone know that
while she was being injected with immunizations she
would receive a tainted batch. From that point on, her
growth was retarded. It was documented that she was
born normal, but about age 2 or 3, she began to show
signs of slowness. By age 4 or 5, it was clear she was
mentally retarded and disabled. Our lives revolved
around Cindy and her need for special care. I never
knew Cindy in any other way, though I should I say--not
in this life. Once and only once have Cindy and I shared
a moment together that we would consider "normal,"
that moment was in the dream world.

Now, as I document the following few words, you may
think how cruel I am. But maybe you have not had a
sibling whose life is controlled, like being a slave to
rules and regulations with no freedom to live her life the

way she might have chosen. Yet I know it is all for her own protection. Someday when it is Cindy's time to pass into Eternity, I am not sure I will be sad. I want her to feel complete and whole, to not be disabled, to make her own choices, to walk on the beach, or up a mountain, to eat a dozen fresh baked cookies or anything thing she wishes.

. . . .

I find myself walking side by side with Cindy. I realize for the first time she really does know who I am and she is content and free of the disabilities that she has carried through this life. We were really talking. (I say that because in this life our conversations consist of toys, clothes, purses, candy, money and food. She is so happy when she can spend a couple of dollars at the dollar store on her little treasures.)

We are walking down a path just happy to be together. Off to my right I see my father-in-law Doug. He is standing and leaning up against a metal bar somewhat like a bike rack. He looks great. The last time I saw him was in the final stages of his battle with cancer. He passed in 1978. Here he has a full head of hair. He looks about forty, standing tall, lean and happy. We each say "hi" to each other. I notice someone standing behind him, a young man of about twenty years old. I look directly at Doug and ask him if this is Dennis's twin brother and he says yes.

I remember that Beth, Dennis's mom, had often told me she had thought that maybe Dennis was a twin.

His name is Stanley but he is called Stan.
He has wavy brown hair, but he is not an identical twin.

Over off to my left, is my Dad. Cindy and I walk over to him and we literally get inches away. We, as in Dad and me, both said something like, "It's been a long time." He looked so awesome, so vibrant. If I had to guess his age it would be forty-five. He and Cindy hugged and she called him "Daddy-sun." I remember thinking this is what she used to call him when she was a child. Upon waking, I do not recall if she actually did it or not as a child, but felt confident that she had.

Again, I look off to the side and see Jared and Matt. Cindy and I both grab Jared and attempt to hold onto him forever. After a few moments, we do release our grip and relax. I take a step back and see Matt.

I remember that a few visits ago Matt had teased me about his name. I find myself, becoming playfully aggressive and I sternly and lovingly take my hand, and kind of lightly smack him and sternly ask, "So what is your name?" He said, "Matthew _ _ _ _ _ Miller." I lose track of the various middle names he had said only knowing that one of them was Stone, but mostly everyone calls him, Matt.

He said Matthew was pronounced a little different

somewhat like, "Matthern."

Suddenly, I see movement a few feet behind him and I wonder is this Michael, but I do not know.

May every sunrise,

hold more promise,

every moonrise

hold more peace.

anounymous

August 10, 2007
Matt & Michael

. . . .

This seems so odd. It's been years since I have been to
St. Vincent Church, but that is right where I now find
myself sitting. (If you walked in the main entrance at
the back and walked towards the front, I am the one
sitting about ten rows up on the left, wondering, "How
did I get here?")

. . . .

*I grew up in this church and the adjacent school. Some
of my fondest memories happened at this school and
church. I spent eight years of my childhood here. In the
1960's the school ran two classrooms per grade. Most
of the teachers were nuns with a couple of lay teachers.
In those days, you could get a pink slip for walking on
the grass. In the first grade, the nuns wore full habits
from top to bottom. I do not know the correct term for
the headwear, but it did consist of a shield of sorts, like a
visor around the whole face that extended maybe two
inches beyond their facial cheekbones. For many years
we never knew if any of them had hair. I do not recall
what year things began to relax. I do know by the sixth
grade the nuns wore skirts and blouses with sweaters*

and that the skirts were just a touch below the knees. So finally we knew, they were just as human as the rest of us.

. . . .

So here I am, with my father-in-law Doug. He looks healthy, happy and vibrant. We talk for quite a bit, but of course all I remember is that he said, "Look for Raymond."

This makes no sense as I only know one Raymond who happens to be a cousin. I feel like this is a clue to something. I frantically, start looking around to make sense of this odd little clue. I stop and I notice someone whose name is Raymond, but I do not personally know him. He is a television actor, whose name is Raymond. In an instant I am over where he is. *Wait a second, how did I move so fast in just a second or two?* Now, I am on the right side of the church about half way up and Raymond is gone.

Sitting on the pew behind me are two young men. As I turn, I am standing up and I realize one of them is Matt. I also notice that they are seated side by side. They are almost alike, both pretty close to identical, yet I can tell the difference. They each have a shaggy haircut maybe an inch off the shoulder. I think they are both wearing braces. I only notice because they are smiling so big.

One of them says to me, (and I believe it was Michael), "Can you guess which one of us is Matt?" I look left to right and right to left, and I know Matt is seated on the left. I respond, "Matt is on the left." This is the first time I see them side by side.

. . . .

Suddenly I am awake. I finally realize for the first time that it is Matt and Michael. There really are two of them. When I have sensed someone else, unsure of who else was there, I now know it was Michael! I am filled with a sense of joy and overwhelming peace and desire to know my boys.

I wait for the Lord,

my soul waits,

and in His word

I put my hope.

Psalm 130:5

August 12, 2007
My friend Dottie

. . . .

My dream and my desire, for my life has been to be able
to help people in need of assistance. If only I had the
resources, I think I would be spending my days
supplying the needs of the many. I have always felt like
that was what I am to do.

. . . .

So here I am doing that in the dream world. My
husband and I seem to be in charge of a help site, a
facility for life's refugees with all sorts of problems. The
people are hungry. They need jobs, housing, clothing,
friendship and a safe and warm place to rest. The list
could go on and on. I am amazed how the clients appear
to be patiently waiting, knowing that in time their needs
will be attended to. Time does not seem to matter as
they contentedly wait. The room has a sense of serenity
and calm.

Dennis has stepped out for a moment when the phone rings. I answer with a simple, "Hello."

The caller says, "Hi! This is Dottie."

I feel stunned and I reply, "DOTTIE?"

She says, "YES DOTTIE."

I say, "No, Dottie is in Heaven, she can't be calling me." She says "YES, this is Dottie from Heaven."

I can hear her voice and I realize that indeed it is my friend Dottie, with her silly sense of humor. After a few sentences have been exchanged, I boldly ask her, "Have you seen Jared?" She responds, no, but they communicate via something like email, and it is called "Mind Mail." They both are so busy they have not had time to visit in person.

. . . .

Here on earth, Dottie watched Jared grow up through her visits at our family store. Jared had loved her silly sense of humor. They loved to flirt with each other, as well as exchange hugs and friendship. It did not matter that there was fifty or sixty years age difference.

When it came to Dottie and her sister Flo, you just felt like old soul friends. Jared and Dottie shared the same birthday so that seemed to add to the fun mix as well.

. . . .

I asked Dottie if she had any messages for her sister Flo as she was still here on this side. Dottie's response was, "Tell Flo to get her hair set." As I realize it indeed is Dottie, I realize how much I miss her silly sense of humor.

. . . .

The next day I wrote a letter to Flo, anxious to tell her about Dottie. Flo responds rapidly. Flo said, "that the last conversation she had with Dottie was all about getting their hair fixed."

Come to me,
all who are weary
and burdened,
and I will give you rest.

Matthew 11:28

February 24, 2008
Dennis has a twin

• • • • • • • • • • • • • • • • • •

I find myself dancing with my niece, Kyndal. She seems younger than she really is. I am aware that I am in a regular dream. Suddenly, my father-in-law Doug, whispers in my ear. I do not see him. I only hear his voice. I ask Kyndal to hush a bit so that I can hear what is being said. He is aware that I can hear him, but it seems odd to hear him and not to see him.

I ask Doug two questions, and this time I remember the answers that he gives.

My first question is, "Can you describe how awesome Jesus is?" He responds, "He is so awesome that I cannot begin to describe Him." Next I ask him, "Does Dennis have a twin?" He responds, "Yes, and his name is Stan."

Even though I have heard these words before, this confirms a previous visit. He also told me that "Jared is always looking over us, watching us, us being his family and that Jared and Jesus would be coming soon to me."

I am guessing that it means in the dream world.

Wherever,

so ever you go,

go,

with all your heart.

Confucis

June 17, 2008
Awesome

· · · · · · · · · · · · · · · · · · · ·

*Sometimes it seems odd when our world collides with
eternity. I am finding it easier to navigate around the
moment, aware of which is which.*

· · · · · · · · · · · · · · · · · · · ·

I am in a room with a man and a woman. They both tell
me that I look familiar to them, so we attempt to narrow
down the connection. No, they do not live in Oregon.
They ask, "Have you been to California?" I respond,
"Yes, a few times to Disneyland, a few times to my
daughter's house and three weeks in Pasadena." They
are from Pasadena. So I begin to describe why I was in
Pasadena for awhile. I was attending the trial of the man
who had been negligent while driving and he had killed
my son. The trial was for the manslaughter charge
against him. It turns out these people were on jury duty
for such a trial, but not sure if it was the one related to
us, but it was about the same time period.

I am now walking down a hallway with another woman.

She is telling me that she can talk to people in heaven. I turn towards her and I comment, "Really? You can talk to people in heaven?" She seems a bit puzzled as to why she has to confirm this, and with a stern voice she replies, "Yes."

We walk into a room that has a table about six feet long. She starts to tell me that, "Jared is here."

She had no idea about me and Jared, yet she makes this statement.

I am now in two different aspects of the dream. Part of me cannot see Jared and yet another part can. As I am conversing with the woman, I find myself next to her and also up in the balcony looking down. It is from the balcony that I first see Jared. I realize that he is aware of both of me. He does not seem confused, but for a moment, I am. I am watching myself down below and I am having a conversation with Jared up high. All the while he remains down low. He still has his silly sense of humor. I know that I ask three or four questions. One was trying to confirm that Matt and Michael are twins, yet I do not remember his responses. Next I ask, "Why don't you come to Dad and Nicole in their dreams?" He said, "They need to grow in their faith a bit more," implying that if they did, he would come.

Next I ask, "How awesome is God?"

As I had asked the question, and I am on the last word,

Jared stands tall and turns around ever so slowly. As he does, he takes on a new appearance. He was totally Jared, my Jared, but now he is translucent and glowing with purity. He spoke with pure knowledge, pride, and confidence.

Jared replied with these words:

"One day I watched God shave, and as He shaved He cut himself and bled. That this bleeding represented God's tears for us." Us, the entire, human race. Every soul that has been created, through all of time."

"For every big and little sorrow, every heartbreak, every thing that we have agonized over mentally and physically, everything that bothers or annoys us. All of this matters to God. He carries and holds it all."

. . . .

For the next few weeks of my life, I felt like I should just hide in a cave, with dark glasses on trying to shield myself from this description of glory. The force behind this power of glory was so awesome. It was whole, complete and true. He is our creator. For days, I felt like I glowed with an amazing bit of knowledge.

As I tried to understand the magnitude of what Jared had said, I slowly began to feel so simple, not yet ready to comprehend what all of it really meant.

For a moment I had felt a particle of his agony and I have become overwhelmed with the weight of what it meant.

Our greatest glory,
is not in never falling,
but in rising
every time we fall

Confucius

November 2008
For a moment, I am complete

• • • • • • • • • • • • • • • • • •

These words begin the written recognition of a visit from December of 2005. I am not sure why it took me so long to place it among the other visits but I finally have. If I have not expressed this clearly, these events happen in the dream world. They are what I believe to be visits from heaven.

I do not recall this dream in much detail, (I don't know why unless that was the way it was meant to be,) because in doing so, I might distract you from the one thing that is magnificent. I was in heaven, in a low-lit setting which made it hard to define my surroundings.

What I do know is that I was hugged by Christ. At no time did I see his face. But I felt alive, whole and complete! One with God--yet still me. I felt the connection that we shall inherit when we each pass to eternity. This will happen after we have completed our journey here on earth. Once I became alert in the awake state, I realized how lonely we really are without this connection. It is beyond any love and connection we have with our loved ones and it surpasses anything we could possibly imagine.

Art washes away
from the soul
the dust of everyday life
Pablo Picasso

December 10, 2008
A glowing face

. . . .

I am walking in a room filled with what seems like forty
or fifty people. A woman who seems younger than me
is approaching and she tells me that she is Minnie, my
mom's mom, Grandma Minnie.

. . . .

*I never had much time to know her as I grew up. I have
always felt like I have missed out on something very
special. She lived in South Dakota while I lived in
Oregon. A family with five kids and one of those kids
having disabilities, made traveling long distance harder
for us than for most. I remember Grandma coming to
visit us once or twice as a child. I may not have many
memories, but I have felt her love and it transcends what
was lacking. She and I played canasta, a card game, for
many hours, laughing and talking. There are times I
find myself envying the cousins who lived near her, as
they really got to know her.*

. . . .

I ask her, "Who are all these people?" She says, "They

are some of our ancestors."

I look up and I see my mom and Aunt Susie across the room.

I'm not sure how I left that room, but now I am at a house or an apartment. I know that this is where Jared lives in heaven. I get the impression he lives here with his brothers. I sense that besides Jared there are three other people here as well. I hear someone say "Mikey." At first I thought I saw Matt, but I am not sure. I see a glowing soft face with shoulder length hair, light brown in color and a well-trimmed beard with a huge smile. He is almost glowing himself, kind of like he has a halo that outlines his body. I do not think it is Matt or Michael, but I know they are here in this room.

Off to the side across the room, Jared sees someone he knows who is still on earth. He smiles ever so happily and calls him by name, "Sammy." Tears of joy fall from Jared's face.

Jared tells me to work harder on getting the camp, "his camp" going. I am also surprised, that Jared appeared older than as I last saw him when he was on this side of eternity. I guess that might be normal as it has been about four and half years since his passing. I tried a few times to ask for a verbal confirmation from Jared, about Matt and Michael being twins, but I get no answer.

As I woke up, I realize who the other person was and I

thought how stupid or ignorant I am. How did I not know? It was Christ.

Our lives begin to end
the day
we become silent
about things that matter.
Martin Luther King

January 6, 2009
Aunts and Uncles

. . . .

It is early in the evening, the sun is setting and just a bit of light still stretches across the heavens. A woman approaches me and she is going to show me around. She tells me that I will meet a few people. We step through the doors of a barn and there are five or six women standing and leaning against a fence that is attached. All of them are facing me. She implies that some of them are sisters of Chris, my Uncle Leo's wife. For some reason I mention that, "I think my Uncle Leo was my Dad's favorite brother."

. . . .

Not sure why I say that, maybe because my Dad watched over him after he had his stroke. I can hardly remember Leo before the stroke. I do remember the day that some of the family gathered at Leo and Chris's house when the stroke overtook him.

. . . .

The woman introduces herself, and if I recall correctly, she said her name was Gladys. I write her name in the palm of my hand.

110

We walk around what seems like a community, and sometime during the walk she is no longer with me. Now my Aunt Clara is here. We hug and continue walking.

We enter a room and there is a young man there. I would guess he is in his late twenties. He has shoulder length hair.

I look directly at him and I say, "Please tell me the truth and don't tease me. Are you Matt?" He says, "Yes." I ask about another brother and he asks me, "Do you want three sons?"

I quickly and sternly respond, "Yes." He does not confirm or deny the twin assumption that I have had for some time. I wonder, why would he ask this? I would love any amount of children I had.

Suddenly Matt is blushing and seems embarrassed. He says to me, "Remember the loft apartment, the one before you got married." (Dennis had a loft apartment.) He implies that I was pregnant there.

· ·

I have always had really hard menstrual cycles. I suppose it could be possible and I did not know.

· ·

Clara and I continue to walk. We enter yet another room. There is a bed with someone sleeping under the covers. They are totally covered so I cannot tell who it is. Next to the bed is a baby bassinet, with a beautiful sweet baby laying there. Clara is purposely nudging me towards the bassinet until I am touching it with my leg. The baby is fussing and I am encouraged to pick it up. The baby seems a little smaller than normal and it is wrapped in a receiving blanket. I gently pick the child up, cradling it in my arms. A photograph is taped or attached to the front on the blanket. It is a picture of my daughter Nicole. I think it is her first grade picture, the one with the cute red plaid dress. It is implied that Nicole has tiny faith but it will grow.

Follow the way of love

1 Corinthians 14:1

January 2009
A Spiritual Cleansing

· ·

Today I had spent the afternoon as a chaperon for a
group of children. We were guests at a museum learning
center. Our trip was complete and everyone headed for
the bus to return us home. I jumped off the bus for what
I expected to be a moment to find something that was
left behind. The children are getting on the bus and I
assume that I have enough time. Apparently the driver
was not aware that I had left for a few seconds, so he left
without me. I knew that the children will be fine as I
know we had quite a few adult chaperones.

I am back inside the building we all had just been to, but
now I am being held against my will or maybe even
confined, yet free to wander around. I am walking
around talking to others, trying to figure out what is
going on. Why, am I here and why am I not allowed to
leave? It is not a bad place. It even seems like a place
filled with serenity and calm. It feels like I have spent
quite a few hours here wandering and talking.

I discover that this place is a place to grow, to learn, to
meditate, to find peace, to let go of stress, to let go of
issues and baggage. I cannot say what I might have

learned, only that upon waking I felt a huge spiritual cleansing. I am peaceful and calm. I even felt a bit pure. I felt purged of things that are irritations to me and now I am somewhat peaceful. Some of the heartbreak I carry had been released.

Do you hear
the echo of the mountains,
listen for
the trickle of wonder in the stream,
feel the roar of
His glory in the waterfalls
Let His essence calm you.

Vickie Miller

February 23, 2009
My son's are home

• • • • • • • • • • • • • • • •

I am sitting on my bed facing the door and I am having a conversation with Jared. Though, again I do not remember the words only that I know they were spoken.

I open the double doors and Jared joins Matt and Michael who are whizzing by. They are all in such a hurry, heading towards the laundry room and outside.

Wow! This is the first time that I am really aware that Matt and Michael were in our family home. I get up and proceed to follow them. I realize that even though we have not seen them here in our home, that they know where their home and family are.

Outside there are ten or so people sitting on my front lawn. Everyone is watching my neighbor dig a trench along the west side of my house. It all seems like it should be, I just don't know exactly why the trench is being dug.

I go back into my house and things seem a bit different. The hall and laundry room are the same. The bathroom and bedroom are the same but as I walk a step or two into the kitchen area, I realize that the cabinets are cherry-wood not oak. Also, the layout of the kitchen is sort of half reversed. A young lady is sitting at the table eating cereal. She looks at me and implies that she might be my daughter and that her name is Elizabeth, but everyone calls her Lizzy.

May we wish to soar with the eagles,
and fly
on the wings of peace.
May the birds' chirps
bring joy to your ears
and simplicity into your heart

Vickie Miller

Me & Mom
May 3, 4, 5, 2009

. . . .

May 3

I am in the house that I spent half my childhood in on 4th Avenue. I am heading to the dining room to exit out the door onto the deck, down the stairs towards the backyard. I am thinking that old walnut tree sure has been here a long time, and thinking about our little white puppy, Cody. He wasn't very large so he always seemed more like a puppy. He was sweet and gentle.

The tree branches have become overgrown and hang down low, and I seem to have to jump over a few. I loved the shade the tree provided. It was a pretty tree, but it was such a messy tree as well.

. . . .

Thinking back to my teen years, I remember trying to not be available when it was walnut time. The pods were such a black icky mess. The black goo would get on my hands and under my fingernails. Looking back I think my brothers and I did a good job of avoiding helping mom with the chore. Though I do remember a few times getting stuck with picking them up off the ground and

*placing them in the garage. Mom would spend hours
pulling the pod off from the shell, cracking and digging
out the nut. It was almost like a jewel to her. She would
not waste any of the gems. The oven was fired up for it
was the method of drying the little jewels. Mom would
bag them and then freeze them.*

. . . .

I keep walking towards the west and turn south along the
deck as I know Mom is outside on the south side of the
house gardening. As I start to make the turn, there is my
mom (she had passed a year earlier). She is down on
hands and knees digging in the dirt, working it with her
hands and planting the most vibrant red and yellow
flowers that I have ever seen. The flowers themselves
caught my interest as they seemed full of energy,
glowing with color and pulsing with an essence. Mom is
thin and young, looking about forty. When she passed,
she was in her eighties.

I said to her, 'See I told you that you would be young
and healthy in heaven." She looked at me and smiled.

May 4

Mom and I are standing across the street from our 4th
Avenue house looking west towards our house. I am
telling my mom that maybe someday I would buy the
house back and turn it into a home for young teens who
are pregnant and who have no support from their own

families. (My heart breaks for kids who find themselves in this type of a situation and no one they can count on.) She likes the idea but she also makes a suggestion of, "maybe a home for people like Cindy with brain damage."

May 5

I am with Mom, Dad, Jared, Aunt Pat, Doug and someone else who does not make themself known. We are all walking and talking. Only one sentence was recalled upon waking. My father-in-law, Doug, told me that Jared follows me around a lot and that he is always checking up on me.

He alone

stretches, out the heavens,

and

treads on the waves of the sea

Job 9:8

December 31, 2009
For my friend Richard

. . . .

Today I am at my place of business. I am standing at the
main counter and customers are wandering around our
store. My friend, Richard, is standing close by and we
are chatting. A young man is with him and he has his
arm draped over his shoulders. I should mention that
this young man is somewhat translucent or invisible to
all others except me and that Richard is not aware of his
presence.

The young man is about twenty-five years old and two
or three inches taller than Richard. He has dark hair and
a moustache and he is glowing with pride and love. He
implies that Richard is his Dad. He is "aware" of all that
his Dad has done for him. He knows how much his Dad
loves him and that he is proud to be his son. I can feel
the pulse of the overwhelming love that this young man
has for his father and the depth of the emotion.

I am trying to tell Richard about this young man
standing next to him. Yet he is still unaware of his
presence. As I am trying to describe him to Richard, I
refer to the height and weight of Thomas, the brother of
one of my employees.

A few days later I see Richard in person in the awake

state. As I tell him about the dream visit, he does not recall any of the happenings. By the time I was done telling the story he was all but in tears. I believe he felt joy as he realized his son is aware of all that he does for him.

(Richard's son is disabled and not able to communicate clearly to all.)

Life itself

Is,

the most wonderful,

fairytale of all

Hans Christian Andersen

February 14th, 2010
Confirmation of twins

• • • • • • • • • • • • • • • • • • • •

I am starting to realize the harder I try to stay in the
moment that I cannot. I need to relax and try to remain
calm while having the visits. Not so easy when you hope
to have visits with the people that have passed to eternity
and especially when it is your child or children.

Today's visitor is a woman who looks about twenty-five.
Her hair is pulled up in an old style bun, something like
the way women wore their hair a hundred years ago.

I find myself thinking and saying, "You sure look like a
younger version of my Dad's mom, Grandma Brown-
Burgard." I am thinking it is odd how my Dad's mom
was always referred to by her last name and not her first.
She says that she is Grandma Schuchardt. She is my
great grandmother on my mom's side of the family.
Though she is familiar, I do not know her, other than
through the genealogy research I have done and the
pictures I have compiled. I really have no photos of her
before about age fifty, so I trust she is who she says she
is.

I ask her, "Do you know how Jared, is?" She says or
implies, "He is so great, so happy."

127

I ask about Matt and Michael, "Are they twins?" She says, "Yes." When she responded she had an attitude about her that caught my attention. Though it was nice, it was like, don't you get it already. "They are twins." How many times do you need confirmation?

I also had a feeling that my Aunt Pat was in the background. Moments later I was with Aunt Pat in her dwelling in heaven. I remember two walls being painted with all roses.

My love for you,
is a journey,
Starting at forever
And ending at never

anonymous

John
February 2010

. . . .

*I can't begin to understand why someone famous or
shall I say a celebrity might visit me, but he did. My
guess is that many times I have felt close to being
defeated, not sure if I can hang on one more day. It is
not so easy to place your child in a box and bury him.*

. . . .

I am unsure of where I am, just that it is a large meeting
hall, a gathering place for events. The celebrity is
someone most of us know of though he has been gone
for some time. This person has asked me to help with
his planned demonstration for the day. He will be
showing an audience how to tie ropes and do rope tricks.
Today I met, John Wayne.

During the course of the demonstration, John and I are
having a real conversation. He asks me which of his
movies is my favorite? I say, "I cannot remember the
title, but it had a famous football player in the movie,
playing his adopted Native American son." He asks me
what did I think of his Alamo movie, did I like it? I said,
"Yes, it was good, but the other one was still my

favorite." He asked me what do I collect, and "I said teddy bears, but that I had given most of my collection to the Starbucks Christmas Toy Drive. He picks up a phone and orders something of a teddy bear nature.

I tell him that my best friend in high school, Terri, was a huge fan of his and that she had movie posters of him in her bedroom.

As the demo proceeds, I see my daughter and one of her friends in their, Girl Scout uniforms. They look to be about in the sixth grade. (I am thinking this can't be.)

It is the year, 2010, the girls are in their thirties. I ask someone in the audience what year is it, and they say 1963. I keep saying, "no it is 2010."

Upon waking I feel like that I have met John Wayne. He had a gentleness, wholeness and completeness about him. He was happy.

A few days later I realize the movie that I was trying to recall was, *The Undefeated.*

Hope
is a waking dream

Aristotle

• •

As I walk towards the doors of a large gathering hall, I see my aunts, Susie and Clara seated by the door entrance. Someone else is also behind them, her face is hidden from my view. I can feel her presence, and I know that it is Dee. Delores is one of my first cousins and she had died a few days ago. So today on earth we gather for her memorial service and in eternity they gather as well.

I stop in front of my aunts and I say, "You guys look so young and beautiful."

Almost in tune with one another they both start teasing me, saying, "Didn't you think that we were young and beautiful, on earth in your time?" I find myself embarrassed as I try to withdraw and back pedal trying to not insult them.

They are so totally teasing me. In an instant, I realize that it is I who now is the old one. When my aunts passed they were both in their eighties. Here I am old at fifty three.

As I step forward, I realize that the gathering hall is filled with people, all of whom are dressed in shades of black and grey. I look around for a bit, knowing my mom and dad will be here, but I am unable to locate them.

Wisdom

begins in wonder

Socrates

Christmas Morning
In the Library
2010

. . . .

I haven't been to this library before. I can't tell you
where it is located, but it seems to have walls and walls
of books. Not uncommon for a library, it kind of
reminds me of where the Salem Library was when I was
a child in the 1960's, an old house in our downtown
core. I am walking down a flight of stairs and I am
drawn into a room.

I hear what sounds like a musical card or a music box
playing a lovely song. I get a sense that the woman
nearby just might be my mom. She had taken a book off
the shelf and laid it down and walked away.

I am thinking, why won't this book stop playing music?"
It will not stop. With a determined step, I walk towards
the book knowing all I have to do is to close the cover
and it will stop. I bend over to grab the book and I see
the numbers 147 engraved on the cover.   I am thinking,
How odd. Am I in a regular dream or a dream visit?"

Just last night my brothers Tim and Clark, and I were discussing our Dad's regiment in World War II. He was with the 147th regiment out of Aberdeen, South Dakota.

I sense someone else who I believe is of the male gender and he has long hair. I see a glimpse of a face, soft and out of focus and I realize who He is. I stand and I am in awe as I realize He is the Lord Christ.

Suddenly He is across the room with Dennis, my husband. Dennis is now as white as a sheet, glowing as he stands next to the Lord, totally speechless as he realizes who is near him. A man approaches Dennis. He seems to think that Dennis knows something and he wants to know what it is. He just won't stop until he figures it out. Dennis somehow went to another room and I am watching him trying to tell a group of people about who he just saw. He rises and stands in front of a mirror. As he faces the glass, I see another image reflecting off the surface. I know who He is.

Upon waking I creep quietly out of the bedroom just in case Dennis is aware and knows that he is in this dream. I do not want to wake him before he is ready. Once he is awake he has no recollection, but I know that he and the Lord were together.

A few minutes later I pick up the devotional book that I have been reading and randomly open it to the page with the date of June 2.

. . . .

The book title is, "God Calling" and the subject of the daily devotional is titled "my image." A few lines into the reading it says, "that no man can see my face and live." And upon the soul becomes stamped, my image."

First keep the peace
within yourself,
then
you can also bring
peace to others

Thomas a Kempis

The Escalator – Purgatory
January 30, 2011

. . . .

I find myself in a large room, maybe a school gymnasium or a bowling alley. Immediately I am scanning and searching the room, looking for someone or something that is familiar. I see Jared. Instantly I am near him.

When I say scanning the room, it is an odd sensation. It's a thought process of searching for someone's aura, a sensing of their presence. It is like our brain has another skill that we here on earth have not yet developed in this present state of our evolution. In no way is it intrusive. At no time have I ever felt violated or intruded upon with any of these mind senses I have experienced. It is another sense we have once we pass to eternity, just like hearing, taste, smell and touch.

Jared is dressed in long pants and a t-shirt with a fleece vest jacket. He is standing with his arms crossed and has the biggest smile ever. It was his smile that caught my eye first as I was scanning the room. He tells me that he is great and I ask him, "Are they twins?" And he says, "Yes." I ask about Lizzie and he says, "No." Yet again I am confused. I ask about God, something like how awesome is he? He responds, "He is so awesome!" I realize in a past visit I had asked the same question and got a perfect answer with the story of God shaving.

I begin to quickly look around the room searching for my parents, but I do not sense them. Nicole, my daughter, is with me. She is heading across the room to an activity area. It is like a school carnival where I see balls tossing and people dropping into a water tank.

We both stop and look at a man just standing here and together in unison we both say, "That's Mickey Mantle."

I am thinking, "Wow, really!"

Nicole gets in line to play the game of tossing the ball. She wins the toss, but no one drops into the water. I know that in winning that game she is safe. She walks back to me to show me a baseball with Mickey Mantle's name engraved or imprinted on it. I sense the texture almost like it is alive. She returns for a second game.

As Nicole continues playing the game, I find that I am going down some escalators with two of Nicole's friends. We figure we might have a better vantage point to view the games from a different angle. Halfway down I realize that there is no return on these stairs. Once I reach the bottom I see Nicole thinking about getting on and following us down. I sternly yell at her, "DO NOT COME DOWN. DO NOT FOLLOW ME."

As I look up, she stops. Now there is a wall of blackness. Those of us who have come down cannot see up. Thankfully, she did not follow. I realize that this is a place of limbo, something like purgatory. Nicole's two friends begin to panic and are running around frantically; they feel trapped and scared. A little critter the size of a baby kitten is chasing them and they are afraid. Over and over, endlessly, they run in circles.

I realize that I am allowed down here to observe what is going on. I relax because I know this, and I begin to look for the exit. I am an observer who will return above to tell others.

Most of the people are absorbed in what appears to be playing video games, consumed with the game much like when we might play a computer solitaire over and over, or just one more row in crocheting or knitting, just one more. This place revolves around people stuck in this endless loop, addictions of sorts.

I sense (or know) that I am to tell them and you, "just stop, hold, your head up, lift your thoughts and think of someone else. Reach for the heavens. Think of a good deed and do it. Raise your awareness to something greater than us. Look for our Creator. Find solitude in nature. Observe the birds and flowers. Climb the trails and mountains. Watch a child play. Sing a song. Whistle a tune. Look at the face of a baby. Thank God for creating you. Open your heart to another. Stop and for a moment, just breathe and relax and try to visualize our awesome God of creation.

. . . .

Someday, we will realize that there is something greater than ourselves, and out of this purgatory we will walk.

. . . .

I take notice of a sign slightly pointed upward, with an arrow painted on it. A few others notice it as well. As we wait for our turn to proceed forward and upward, they have found a sense of joy realizing all they had to do was to open their hearts and eyes to our Creator.

. . . .

So again I have found another answer to my question of how awesome God is.

*All truths
are easy to understand,
once they are discovered;
the point is to discover them.*

Galileo Galilei

May 3, 2010
Wisdom to be given

• • • • • • • • • • • • • • • • • • •

I am here, but am not sure where "here" is. Some of my aunts are here, Susie and Clara, a cousin's wife, and my Mom. A few others are hanging around, but I cannot say for sure who they are.

My mom is mumbling like she has no teeth. She says two or three sentences but I can not understand the words.

• • • • • • • • • • • • • • • • • •

This reminds me of the day before she died. She tried to tell me something. But then, too, her words were mumbled. I knew her words must have been important because she woke from a coma-like state to say them.

The only thing I did understand was her request for water. I still wonder, "What she was trying to tell me? Was it that Jared and Dad were waiting for her? Was she saying goodbye? Was she saying she had a glimpse of heaven? Was she saying she was not afraid?"

I can tell you, that day, something else happened. As I have said before, I have a sister, Cindy, who is mentally

145

disabled. Well, that day Cindy came for a visit. While her caretaker was conversing with one of my brothers I followed her around. You never knew what she might take that was not hers, or what she might do. She looked at mom and said, "Mommy sleeping." I said, "Yes, mommy is sleeping,"

She headed towards the bathroom and she stopped and looked at me and said, "Daddy is crying."

I was not expecting that and I said, "What?" She again said, "Daddy is crying." I asked her, "Was daddy happy or sad?" With a, "don't you get it attitude," she replied, "Daddy is in heaven and he is crying."

If you have ever met Cindy, you would know she could never make this up, let alone complete a sentence like this. I believe my dad as well as grandparents, and my sons must have been waiting for mom to make the step from her earthly life into eternity.

. . . .

Clara and Susie are standing nearby. They speak in my mind and they say, "It will be long before your flame extinguishes here on earth, you have much to do and much wisdom will be given." Something else was implied about a child to be given, and I said I could not have any more children. They laughed and said, "God could do anything."

I asked about Jared. They said he was off doing much important work. I knew they must think why, does she keep asking about Jared? I assumed Susie would understand, as she too had lost a son and had to continue her life without him for many years.

Unless you believe,
you will not
understand

Saint Augustine

February 2011
Heaven & Earth side by side

• •

I am a passenger in a van, driving west on Lockhaven Drive. We have just passed the Dairy Queen where the slight little slope or hill in the road begins to level out. Off to the right I get a view of Staats Lake with the private walking paths intended for the homes around the Lake, but something looks different from afar. As the vehicle I am riding in gets a bit closer, I realize it is the same place as always, but a new dimension has appeared. The housing around the lake is now of European design, maybe even Italian, looking like pictures you might see in a travel or tourism magazine. I realize I am seeing another dimension or vibration of another village on top of what I normally would see.

Two different settings in the same spot playing out two different timelines in current time, maybe one on earth and one in eternity, side by side. The new view has the most vibrant colors and is almost picture perfect. It is serene and peaceful and it feels like nature and time working in harmony.

As I look to the left, where a mobile home park stands, it too is the same, but different. Now instead of mobile homes, there are various buildings. One of them houses a gallery, full of photographs taken by Dennis, all of what his eye loves in nature. He has arrived in heaven before me and I only know this because he and my sons await my arrival in the future.

I wander around a bit looking at the pictures admiring his work and Michael walks past me carrying some of Dennis's work. He is in a hurry, helping Dennis and others to get ready for an exhibit. I see him but it just takes me a couple of seconds to realize it is him, almost like a delayed response. I am not sure he even saw me, at least that is how it seems, but I know he did.

Hold faithfulness
and sincerity
as
first principles

Confucius

June 7, 2011
A conversation with dad

. . . .

My dad and I are walking. Mom is there but she is
slightly behind us, walking in dad's shadow. I'm not
sure why, but she does not come out in front. As of yet,
she does not come close to me in the dream visits. I am
holding my brother Mick, only he is a baby now, here in
the dream world. In life he is eleven months older than
me. This is the first time that I have really seen him
happy. Usually he is somewhat somber.

I ask Dad about Jared, and Dad replies, "He is off doing
something important."

I discuss with my Dad that most of my life, probably
back to my twenties, I have felt like I was going to be
doing something important in my life and that avenue or
path would appear unexpectedly, as in the form of an
inheritance. I asked for this feeling to be removed if it
was not true, but today it still is there.

Dad did say, Jared would be coming back from heaven
to help me build his camp, Jared's Camp. It was implied
that I would see him and that others would not. He was
to be my guide for this work that God wished me to do.

In dreams and in love,

There are no impossibilities

James Arany

June 30, 2011
Five times God protected me from harm

. . . .

I find myself at my brother, Tim's house. It is not the one that I am familiar with, but a newer one. He, Julie and the kids are running around getting ready for something. When the door needs to be answered, it is I who does it. Everything is different, but I know it is their house.

A man is on the front porch wanting to talk to Tim. I tell him three or four times that Tim is not available. Finally, I am so frustrated at this person that I agree to get Tim. When Tim and I return, the man is extremely upset and blames me for all the water across the yard and neighborhood. He implies that if I had gotten Tim sooner none of this would have happened.

Suddenly, I am off the porch and around back, down a bit from the main house, and in a room with a large group of people I do not know. I would guess there are about 100 people, all of the same religious denomination. I am in front of this group standing on a low riser speaking to them.

I am trying to speak loud enough to be heard by all, but their volume seems to be a bit louder than mine. I am trying to tell them that they need to stop elevating themselves to God's level. They are not equal to Him. That the fear of God, is us, humanity realizing how awesome God is, understanding that He is our completeness, our Creator, our Father.

Each time I attempt to get this message across, small factions of the group break away and realize that they have been led astray. They have been blinded by levels of authority within their denomination. These small groups realize the mistake and stand behind me. During the course of these interactions, the larger group attempts to silence me. They try five times and each time I am shielded by God. He protects me and I know no harm will happen. Each time I speak, more and more of the group breaks away, and again others attempt to silence me. These small groups see the energy field protecting me, a miracle of God, who is speaking to them through me. I continue to speak of religions, that no one entity has it right. Many have it partly right, some are quite wrong, some are too full of themselves and that "No One" has it all right. We of the human race need to become less self-absorbed and need to turn our thoughts, dreams, hopes and desire towards loving all of the human race, to remove the barriers we have placed in our lives based on religion, skin color, ethnic background, poverty level and education status.

*Go confidently
in the direction of your dreams,
live the life you have imagined*

Henry David Thoreau

2011
Carrying the cross

. . . .

I find myself outside of McNary High School. I am standing in the parking lot, facing the front of the building. I am looking at a new, beautiful, sand-blasted monument with Jared's name etched into its core. For a moment or two, I stand alone, when guess who shows up? Jared! Of course, we talk for a moment or two, and then we begin to walk slightly west and then north, making our way to the back entrance onto, Lockhaven Drive.

As we are walking, I seem to have a large, white board, about the size of a surf board, tucked under my arm. It seems to be about fifteen to twenty feet long. While we are walking through the parking lot, we talk the whole time. I am still the one carrying the board. It does not seem odd. It is just the way it is.

Jared says a few things to me. I do not remember all the exact words, but he did say something like, he will be coming back from heaven to help me build his camp,

157

and to help me complete other tasks, that he will be my guide from God. He tells me that when this happens, I will be the only one, to hear him, see him, and that others will not.

I often wonder will I ever be able to find the path to completing Jared's hope of building a camp for kids. At times every direction we attempt to take has a road block. It eats at my heart and thoughts that I have not accomplished this assignment.

We reach the barrier where one more step will separate us from the parking lot and the road. As I take the step out of the parking lot into the street, Jared begins to help me with carrying the board. The weight is now equal and the load feels much easier to handle. Though while I carried it alone I felt like I could manage, but when help arrived I felt this huge relief. With his help, much stress is released and calmness begins to settle in. Suddenly the board that seemed like a surf board appeared to be more like a cross.

We turn left and head west towards the river which is the way home as well. As we get close to the intersection at Lockhaven and Windsor, Jared says something about someday, "Let's go back to the old neighborhood on Golden and check it out." We make a right turn onto Windsor heading north instead of south and it seems that I now live north, down a few blocks. All I really remember is lots of stonework on the front of the house and that it seems to be a two-story.

All sorts of people are at our house getting ready for a production of a movie on how my son inspired youth, how his leadership, gentleness, sweetness, friendship and love of mankind inspired others to reach for such goals in their own lives.

Love is a canvas,

furnished

by nature

and

embroidered by imagination

Voltaire

July 23, 2011
Face to face with God

· ·

My dad is sitting next to his brother Leo and his wife Chris. I walk towards them and I sit next to Chris. She says six or seven sentences, but upon waking I don't remember the contents of them.

I recall that while she was on earth I never had much of a chance to know her. Mostly it was because I could not understand her words. I seem to recall that she had a form of Parkinson's Disease. From what I could tell, it seemed to affect her speech the most. I knew that I could not understand any of her words. As I look back I think I was afraid to get too close, so I did not make an attempt to know her or to understand what she might have ever said. Pondering those childhood days, I think I was selfish because I am guessing she was a gentle and interesting person.

My Uncle Leo did not say a word. He just sat and watched us. Dad, Leo and Chris are all happy and content--almost ageless. My Dad looked across the room and implied that my mom was over there and that she was more beautiful than ever.

Suddenly five young men are standing in front of me, left to right. They slowly merged into a line one behind the other. I saw their faces and realized that they were not my son's. What I did know was they were five different personalities or aspects or concepts of God, of Christ.

Somewhere out of nowhere I made a statement. I said, "I thought it was said that no man could see the face of God and live?"

They all smiled, and lightly chuckled. I notice that their hair glowed with a light brownish color. I felt, their/his, love for me. I was loved just for me, just the way I am, flaws and all. That He was pleased with me and all the times I kick myself, aching for the presence of the Lord.

Upon waking I do not recall what the face of the Lord looked like, but for a bit I felt the essence of mass serenity.

Love is

the beauty of the soul

Saint Augustine

September 7, 2011
Mom's house

. . . .

Growing up, I never felt extremely close to my mom, and it is something I had always hoped for. As she neared the end of her life on earth, I finally accepted that it would have to happen in eternity. I did try to always be there for her if I was needed, but I always felt like I had missed out on something. After her passing, I discovered a bit of information about my birth that might have had a bearing on our relationship. One day when discussing this with a second cousin, she told me a story, told to her by her mother. When I was born at the end of 1956, two months premature and only two pounds, I spent five weeks in an incubator. My parents were told to go home and not to bond with me, that I was going to die.

. . . .

Today it has been a few years since my mom's passing and she has come for another visit. My mom has a home in heaven and it is similar to the last home she had here on earth. She has an assortment of trinkets on the tables and shelves and various paintings on the walls. She and I start to have this odd conversation. She seems so alive.

I tell her that we will need to contact the Social Security people because she will need the money to live on. It sounds dumb and I know this. She tells me "to stop worrying about money because it is not needed in heaven."

I notice that she has continued with watercolor painting. She has paintings that are in different phases of completion. Some are on the walls, some on the floor and some on easels. One is with cats and dogs and one or two have flower designs.

She starts to show me some photographs of people I have never seen and she informs me that they are family members, ancestors of ours.

. . . .

Upon waking, I feel such an odd sensation. It takes a moment and I realize it is her pride and love for me. I knew it had been there but I have never felt its essence.

. . . .

Of all the music
that reached farthest into
heaven,
it is the beating
of a loving heart

Henry Ward Beecher

My Parents Pride
2012

. . . .

I am dancing around a room, in a recital. All the dancers seem to be displaying their talents in a way that seems to be a freestyle form of dance.

There are many spectators all seated around the dance floor.

I am having a wonderful time yet I do not see anyone I know.

Though, I do know that my parents are in the audience watching. I can feel their presence and I know that they are seated side by side.

I can also feel their overwhelming sense of joy, and the pride and love they have for me.

*Joy may you have
and gentle hearts content*

Edmund Spencer

Encouragement from the Heavens
June 2012

• •

I find myself replaying my life, living in an old apartment, wondering how we lost our house and got stuck back in this apartment.

After what seems like quite some time, I am somewhere new. As I walk into the new setting, I see my Aunt Lois, Aunt Pat, my Mom and one of their sister-in-laws, Bev. They are all so happy. I see my sons off in the distance, so I continue with my walking though I feel like I should have stopped and talked, but I knew they understood.

Matt, Jared and Michael are sitting on a sofa. All three of them have let their hair grow a bit longer. I notice that it is resting on their shoulders. They are wearing light-colored sports coats and I think Matt has a moustache. As I get closer they are now standing, mingling with a few people. I am looking around the room, and now it seems like 100 or 200 people are here. For the most part I cannot tell who they are, only that I knew them all.

I did sense one specific person, Sister Rosemary, from

my elementary school days. *She is one of the, most gentle souls, that I have ever known and I have thought of her often as I have grown older. She died in a car wreck many years ago.*

All these people are here to let me know that they are supporting and encouraging me, as I attempt to find the path to complete Jared's dream of building a retreat for youth. They are waiting for me and Dennis to lead this project, as it has been hoped for by the Lord.

I remember being sorry and speaking the following words to the Lord, "I'm sorry that I seem to be always looking for my sons." I do not know if He was there but I knew He heard my thoughts. It was an odd feeling as even though I did not see Him, His essence filled the room, so I felt like I could talk to Him, anytime and that I knew He would hear me.

The room was so odd. It had a floor and ceiling, but no walls. The floor was solid and the ceiling was suspended. Though I saw no chains or ropes, it just hovered above.

Lord I do not understand

· · · · · · · · · · · · · · · · · · · ·

Lord I do not understand, what you ask of me,
One moment I know and the next I wonder.

Could you be talking to me?
Really, someone else might be better,
Really, I am lost, I am nothing,
Yet, I long for your presence.

I search for others insight,
How do they know that you are talking,
Some say God told me,
Some say God impressed upon me,
But some, they glow as they have been touched,
Touched, by your hand.

Lord, might you have a moment today,
A moment that you might whisper in my ear
A moment to lightly blow some angel dust upon my path
Just a moment, maybe two or three
Just a moment to sooth my soul
Lord how do I know if you are talking to me.

A weight has settled
It rests heavy on my heart
It is hidden within my eyes

You may not see it, and you may not know of it,
But it is there.
As a tear appears near,
The pain returns to the creases of my face
Thousand of tears have dropped from my soul
My heart is heavy and almost shattered with agony
My thoughts seldom settle,
As my soul aches for one who has gone before me

One day for just a moment or two
I felt an incredible,
Magnificent peace,
For my soul had calmed,
as I recognized a
Warmth had surrounded me,
Touching, my mind, my body, my soul

Proud to call me his child,
The Maker happy with who I am,

I glowed for a time or two,
Though with time it began to dissolve,
I shall remember,
The peace I had felt for a moment or two,
And I knew that I had felt the presence of God.

Vickie Miller

The Trial

The Trial

. . . .

We have all watched various movies and TV shows dramatizing what a courtroom looks like and how all the characters play out their parts. Have you ever been in a courtroom where, somehow, you were connected to what is going on in real life? Maybe you are a witness. Maybe you are in the jury box. Maybe you have a parking or speeding ticket, or maybe you are the defendant in a manslaughter trial. Maybe you might be like me, the mother of a young man who was carelessly killed one day as he made his way up the mountains to help guide and nurture our youth. Yes, most of us, the adults, probably have been in a courtroom.

The jury box feels EMPOWERING! Maybe today I can make a difference. I have the power to decide what is right or wrong.

Sitting in the spectator area, you may feel intimidated, depending on your reason for being here today.

The middle section, with the tables, chairs, computers, documents, lawyers and the defendant, can be downright scary.

There is a judge and she sits up a bit higher. She is presiding over this trial, making sure all is legal and fair.

Everything needs to be done by the book. I get it.

. . . .

The day before the trial began we met with the District Attorney. She had wanted to tell us a bit about the process. She wanted us to have a chance to view the photos that she would be using in the course of the trial. All of the photographs would be shown on a large screen in the courtroom. These photos were part of the evidence. These photos would break your heart as it did ours. It was wise of her to show them to us ahead of time. It gave us a chance to calm down before the trial.

Try to imagine my family and I, the family of the victim, my son, who was killed.

Often during the trial I find myself looking around the room, wondering, is Jared here?

On occasion, I do sense that a jury member or two might be looking at us, watching us, trying to imagine who we are, probably thankful that they are not sitting in our seats.

And then you have the defendant. He arrives every day as he is supposed to. He walks in wearing, khaki slacks and a Hawaiian shirt, loafers, and no socks. He sits in a chair looking smug and bothered, like he had better things to do today, with an attitude like, "Why are we all bothering him?" He is an older man and if I recall correctly in his mid sixties. From my perspective, it appears that he does not feel that he is responsible. His demeanor would indicate that he is not willing to admit his error.

So, here we sit day after day, listening to a replay over and over of a fraction of time that lasts just seconds.

Photos are projected and are displayed largely on the screen, displaying the accident site, the place of my son's death.

The District Attorney called many accident reconstruction experts and emergency personnel to the stand. They spent many hours providing the evidence and facts that painted the picture of what happened.

An off-duty LA, Police Officer was driving the first vehicle around the corner just after the accident happened. His report implied seconds, like two or three, enough to view everything as it rested.

He and his wife immediately jumped into action. She halted the traffic and he attended to my son, trying to save what life might have been left. He saw the placement of the vehicles and all of the debris. Again, there was no doubt as to whose fault this was.

Before the trial began I had met Officer Kim. All I wanted was a hug and to tell him, thank-you for caring for my son, for holding him as he died. As we approached each other I witnessed the tears in his eyes as has asked me, "had we ever found the cross that Jared was surely wearing that day?" All this time later, he remembered our quest.

The DA also called the doctor/autopsy expert who revealed that most of Jared's bones were broken and most major organs were damaged or destroyed beyond repair. My son never had a chance.

Finally, it was time for the defendant to be called to the stand. He swore he would tell the truth and yet, he did not. He avoided taking any responsibility for his actions. At one point the District Attorney asked a straight-forward question. It was clear that there was room on the highway for him to avoid the impact and yet he did not.

She asked, "Why did you not attempt to avoid the impact?" His response was something like this, and I believe it is close to the exact sentence he formed, *"What good would it have done?"*

Try to imagine me, Dennis, Nicole, and Greg, our son-in-law, all seated within hearing distance of this man. We were witnesses to his statement. Instantly our hearts fell through the floor. There was a trap door here today. These words were cold and sharp, words used in a phrase that we may never be able to forget or to put to rest. Today, as I write these words my response is still the same, *"my son might be alive today."*

At this point it did not take long to wrap up the rest of the proceedings. We had barely left the courtroom, heading to the cafeteria in search of beverages when our phone rang. The jury deliberated for one hour and fifteen minutes. Within moments everyone returned to the courtroom. The jury delivered their piece of paper to the Judge. She read it and handed it to the Court Clerk. He proceeded with a verbal reading of the Jury's verdict. As he read it, time seemed to stop, like it was frozen or suspended. We the jury…find the defendant, guilty of manslaughter.

All was quiet for a moment or two.

The Judge gave a date for which we were to return for the sentencing about a month down the road. If we wished, we would be allowed to speak at this time. The defendant would have to listen to our words. Over the last few months, I had little doubt that one day I could speak my thoughts. We returned home to wait, giving us a time to fine tune what we wanted to say.

Writing speeches had never been easy for me, but I was determined that this man needed to feel my pain. I wrote and rewrote my words, hoping Jared and God would be pleased with what I said. If I stayed focused on that aspect, I was pretty sure that when I spoke I would not regret what I had said. I wanted to be direct and confident. I hoped my words would bite just enough in the mind of the defendant. I wanted this man to understand that he killed my son.

After returning home, I was drawn to the garage and the discarded wood scrap pile that Dennis had under his table saw. No, I did not want to go over there. I knew what I was to do. I had this impression placed in my thoughts that I was to make a cross, and that I was to present it to the defendant after I spoke at the sentencing. What does the Lord ask of me? Really, I do not want to do this, and yet here I am picking out two pieces of wood about ten inches long. I lightly sanded them and Dennis helped me notch and glue them together. "Really, I cannot do this." As much as I attempted to fight this thought, it would not leave me. In the end, I knew I had to complete the project.

We returned February 20th for the sentencing. It seemed appropriate that he be sentenced on the same date that Jared had died.

First Nicole spoke. She created a slide show of her brother. She wished to show everyone Jared, her brother, not just Jared, the victim. The Judge, District Attorney, a new public defender and many others were in tears. Clearly everyone knew how she loved her brother and even now in his death he affected others.

Next Dennis spoke. At first he did well, that was until he choose to read a class assignment of Jared's. Jared had written a futuristic letter of where he saw himself in the years down the road. It was a bit too much for him

179

to complete. Nicole rose and approached her dad, helping him complete his words.

Now it was time for me. I had brought a poster picture of Jared. I approached the podium with my speech, the cross and the poster. *It was not until I began to edit these pages that I had reviewed my original notes. Apparently I had blocked out a detail.* I walked past the podium and as I carried my poster, I stopped and turned, facing the defendant. I held my picture up and sternly informed the defendant "that this is my son, my baby, this is who you killed." I stepped back and returned to the podium and continued with my speech. Aside from my slight outburst I believe Jared would have been proud.

At the end of my speech, I told my story of being drawn to the garage and the cross that I had made. It was given to the defendant with words of seeking forgiveness, from the Lord.

Here, now as I write my story, I still struggle with forgiveness. I do know that at some point I have to let go of the anger, because now it is only hurting me.

From all that has been reported to us, it would appear that, on that day he did not set out to hurt anyone. He was careless, but not evil.

What I am really having a hard time with, is his lack of compassion. He has never displayed sadness or sorrow to us. The few words that were directed towards us were more like, echoed feelings of, poor me, I am sorry, I was in the wrong place at the wrong time.

At one point, I almost wrote him a letter telling him, that I was forgiving him. When I began to discuss this with my husband, he hemmed and hawed and began to tell me there was a bit more to the story. There was some information had been hidden from me. It was undisclosed to me, by my husband and daughter, as they were doing their best to protect me. I know that now, but still. Did they not trust me? Did they think I was not capable of handling one more blow? Wasn't it fair that I too should know what they knew? I am now left with wondering what other secret there must be, maybe something else I do not know.

The story had continued without my knowledge.

You see, the man went back to the courts and attempted to have his verdict thrown out. He was unsuccessful. So much for thinking I was ready to send a letter stating some forgiveness. Obviously my thoughts were premature and I shredded the letter I had begun. I doubt he even cares one way or the other if he were to receive any forgiveness from us.

I will probably always struggle with this man's lack of integrity and simple honesty.

....I wonder, has he ever thought twice about Jared....

My words spoken at the Sentencing Hearing:

Your Honor,

I have spent the last three years anticipating this day. It is because of the defendant and the Government that I stand here in this courtroom today. They have forced me and my family as well as Jared's friends into accepting a life without, Jared, by our sides.

Because of the Defendant's actions and the lack of action on behalf of the Government, my son's body is in a box in a graveyard. His spirit, his soul, his true being resides in heaven now.

Many have tried to comfort us with words like, "you know, Jared is in a better place." That may be true, but he is not here with me. Until a person has stood in my shoes do not assume that I really know it's a better place. You try living life without one of your children.

For me as a mother, I always assumed from the instant my child was conceived, that I was here to always protect and nurture them, to watch them grow, to let them spread their wings, to stand back and let them become themselves. I thought I had accomplished this, until the day Jared died and I could not protect him, or hold him, as he slipped from this world into heaven.

The defendant and the Government need to understand that Jared was truly one of those people who made a difference, here in our world. Given the chance he may have prevented many young people from entering this courtroom as a defendant. He knew how to lead, to get the job done and how to turn or guide people down the right path.

Jared had just accepted the Program Director position at Angeles Crest Christian Camp, a youth camp tucked in the mountains not too far from where he was killed. That weekend, that Friday, Jared was headed to that Camp.

Every other week he might have seen a new bunch of youth, ranging from middle school to college. I would guess fifty to one hundred each time. Let's assume Jared would have lived to the age of seventy and that he would have spent twenty five years as a Youth Minister. That each month he would meet and guide 100 people in his workings of Youth Centers and Retreats. If you were to calculate this as I have, Jared would have touched the lives of over thirty thousand people. When you add the ripple affect, just try and imagine how those numbers could have doubled or tripled.

We cannot even begin to truly imagine the impact on their lives he would have made.

Your Honor, a few years ago in September of 2001 a young medical student was driving the I-5 corridor near our home. He was exhausted and fell asleep at the wheel, killing two police officers and injuring one other. This young man was overcome with guilt. He admitted his fault and begged for forgiveness from these families. I admire this young man. I have often thought about writing him a letter and commending him on his actions of accepting responsibility. These are the actions of most humans, but clearly not the defendant.

As we sit in this courtroom, and each of us might think, what would I of done. I can tell you this. That if I know anyone I know my son. My son would of acted with integrity, he would be devastated that he was responsible for the death of another soul;, he would of admitted his guilt and instantly begged for forgiveness, he would of spent the rest of his life trying to make amends for his actions, he would have accepted responsibility and he would of struggled the rest of his days.

I also know Jared well enough to tell you that he has probably forgiven the defendant. You see Jared is a man of integrity, a man of faith, a man you could trust with your life, a man who would open his heart to anyone.

I will admit to being selfish, I have waited for the day to hear Jared's children call me Grandma. The day that Jared would fret over turning forty or fifty, the day I would make fun of his gray hair. You may think that I am just another proud mother, but you just go and ask his friends and teachers, they will tell you the same.

Now, because of the defendant, those days will never come.

Your Honor, it was not until we lost Jared that I could truly understand the words, "all consuming." No parent should ever have to bury a child.

Your Honor, the following words are meant directly for the defendant:

It is ever so obvious that you seek no forgiveness from us, Jared's family. At this point even if you tried the words would mean nothing. You are the word "mystery." The definition is as follows:

Mystery: requires, that we relinguish, an endless search for answers and become willing to not understand.

Recently, I came across a quote by an unknown Tibetan Lama, it reads: We die, not because we are ill, but because we are complete.

At age twenty two, my son Jared was complete, he was ready to enter the gates of heaven. It would appear that you may never be ready. I have tried to grasp why you have no remorse and I cannot.

Do you not, understand the power of these three word

phrases, I am sorry, It, is my fault, I accept
responsibility.

Everything you have said or done, says that Jared's life
did not matter.

When the District Attorney was asking you, why did you
not, use your brakes, why did you not try to avoid the
collision, you said: "What good would it have done".

These words will haunt me forever. My response to your
statement: Maybe Jared would be alive. Maybe you
would not be labeled a killer. It is that simple.

As I can only think of you with total contempt, and at the
same time I cannot understand my own feelings of,
feeling sorry for you.

I strongly suggest that you seek the man behind this
cross. You may find forgiveness there. I do not believe
that in this life that the Miller Family can forgive you.

A different life

. . . .

I had spent the first forty some years of my life just like you and many others. Growing up, getting married, having children.

In 1988, we had the opportunity to start our own business. So, being adventurous, we decided to pursue the prospect. I sit here twenty-five years later, realizing that being in business for oneself is not all that fun. Yes, it sounds impressive. Yes, we got to make many of our choices with no boss hanging over our shoulder. But, most days, all the paperwork went home with me. After dinner when the kids were in bed, you would find me in the office above the garage. We were open six days a week-so not much free time. When there were school functions, I usually took the first chance to go, leaving Dennis behind to handle the business. Now I realize how unfair and somewhat selfish I must have been. At times this business was a burden. Even so, it was a stable job, so it was hard to back away and move on to another occupation. Once we had been self-employed for a few years, it was hard to imagine working for someone else.

Over the years the kids did not seem to mind, though I believe I have heard my daughter later, as an adult, comment once or twice, how she felt it limited all of our free time as a family.

The kids kept busy with, drama, music, dance, marching band and color guard, high school newspaper, Girl Scouts and I am sure a few other activities as well. What family free time we had was usually spent camping and hiking.

We worked Monday through Saturday leaving only Sunday for free time. So like I said, being self-employed was somewhat, time consuming for our family.

So here we are, an average family just having raised our kids and now they both are off getting their adult lives started. Jared is in college in California and Nicole has graduated college. She is returning to the Northwest after a few term jobs with the Nature Conservancy. She is heading to California to start a permanent job with the National Park Service. My kids are happy and thriving in the areas they have chosen. Did I mention how proud we are of both of them?

We all survived the teen years and they are happy young adults making a difference in our society.

I almost forgot-surviving the "terrible two" stage with Jared. It had lasted from about two years to ten years old.   When Jared was about twenty-one, he came to me one day and said, "Mom, remember how you used to tell everyone that I was such a terrible two for so long?" I looked at him and said, "Yes." He chuckled and with his famous smile he acknowledged his past and said, 'Well, I knew I was such an ornery-little shit." I think even in his chuckle he said I'm sorry. He never really went into why, just that he was aware and maybe even purposely doing it. That was all he needed to say. All had been forgiven many years ago. It was just nice to hear him say it out loud.

. . . .

Then one day our lives were turned upside down. A car collision on the Angeles Crest Highway in California was fatal to Jared. It resulted in a manslaughter trial for an old man who was careless.

. . . .

So now we need to figure out how to live the life of grieving parents and how to cope.

After a few weeks, I attempt to resume my work routine. I stayed in the shadows as my employees, two wonderful women, my friends Marsha and Debi, took over much of the work, letting us wander in and out as needed. As I see the baskets full of sympathy cards and flowers that have arrived, I am thankful for Marsha & Debi's ability to keep it together for us. I wonder, but I have never asked, what it was like for them those first few days following Jared's death.   It was apparent that many people came and offered their condolences and support. My guess is Marsha and Debi shared the story over and over and cried many tears with our customers. I am not sure even after all this time if I should dare ask them what it was like.

There are days that I still struggle with barely holding my head up. I do give most of that credit to the Lord. It is He who holds me together. When I am low and barely able to breathe, I talk to Him, in my heart, in my thoughts, but mostly out loud. I ask, "Please Lord, remove some of this anger, some of this stress, some of this sadness. Just bits and pieces, so that I may hold my head up and get through another day. Please! This load I carry is just a bit, too heavy. Please, Lord."

Just about every time I talk to Him, my self-combustion level lowers to a safe place and I can go forward.

Fast forward (a few years) and one day I am driving to work, following my normal path, heading south on Commercial Street, taking the Front Street bypass to avoid all the red lights through the downtown core. As I turn into the curve something happens. The car is full of energy and I am riding along in a bubble of warmth and peace. *Instantly, I knew that our Creator had joined me in the car, and that He is pleased with me and that He loves me just the way I am.* His energy lasted for what would be the time of a two or three block distance at about twenty five miles per hour.

After He left, the warmth remained as I continued my drive to work. This feeling of peace and serenity lasted for about eight more minutes. I knew He had for a moment been in my car with me, calming my essence. ***I had just felt the presence of God!*** I was glowing, what else would you be doing when such a thing happens? It would be a few days later when all the warmth dissolved, and I was left with loneliness again.

As you have read through my dream journal you have been a witness of my story of making a promise to God. You may have even felt the few glimpses of His presence.

So, here I am just like you, but now I have "knowledge," not just faith, but knowledge of such happenings. Making a promise that I am not sure I can live up to yet determined to try. I hope that He will not be disappointed in me if I do not succeed. What I do know is He is pleased with me and who I have become.

I now spend much of my time seeking his presence and searching for a glimpse of His glory. Hoping to find what awaits us in Eternity. Impatiently I wait. There have been many moments I have felt and sensed a presence looking over my shoulder, nudging me right or left, urging me to take another step. I feel incomplete in this life, searching for what makes us one and whole.

As of now, one would think that I might have a glow about me, but I do not. I have knowledge of life beyond.

No longer do I live by faith only, but knowledge as well.

There are parts of the dream world that I have not been able to describe fully, so for that, I feel inadequate in my service to you.

So let me try to describe eternity, heaven and God. It is waiting for each of us.

Peace!

Close your eyes and try to form an image of peace. Slightly tilt your head and face upward, reaching for the skies. You are somewhere bright and warm. The sun's rays make your face glow, almost radiate. Even with your eyelids closed you can see the sun-rays peaking through the clouds. The rays are so intense you stop and think of His Glory and the halo that must surround His entire being. You have a sweet smile on your lips, your muscles are relaxed and nothing aches or itches, no mental or physical pain, just serenity.

You hear this muffled sound. It sounds like a motor in the distance and you are wondering what it is? You turn and slightly open your eyes as you want to peek out, making sure all is well. Remember you are at peace and you are calm. Do not be startled. A few inches in front of your face a hummingbird hovers. You stop and he stops. He is right there looking at you, probably thinking, "they are strange creatures, these humans." Your ears can hear the sound of his flutter, and the sound resembles a soft gentle breeze in your ear, you can even feel the vibration. He is thinking, "She smiled and that was my goal."

As the little bird flies off, you attempt to find peace again. Yet before totally resting in peace, you realize that you did just find peace in a solid form. You think, "Wow, that just made my day."

Again, concentrate on the sun-rays hitting your face. You feel the heat and warmth. You are calm, almost like you are wrapped in a bubble. You are complete, one with joy and peace. A warm and determined breeze becomes a bit more intense and suddenly you sense that someone is near you, right next to you. You do not open your eyes for fear this feeling will dissolve. You feel serene. Time has stopped and your whole core is at peace. You are complete, perfect in the eyes of our Maker. Nothing else matters at this moment. With His touch, all the baggage you harbor is gone. You are free.

As this moment becomes stronger, you realize who He is, and you are thankful for a glimpse of what is to come. The possibilities are endless and Eternity awaits each of us. This is "Awe." It is beyond wonder. You are complete in the eyes of the Lord.

. . . .

I wish to challenge you to seek God with all your heart.

What if tomorrow you wake up a new and improved you, at about thirty years of age, forever? Your back stands up straight and does not ache, your knees do not creak, and you have physical strength to walk for miles, untouched by fatigue with energy to just keep going.

What if, your walking companion is someone with knowledge so vast, so supreme and yet He has all the time and desire to spend every moment with you? He would answer any question and you would be content.

And at the end of the day when you get home, you could sit in front of a campfire with friends and family. You laugh and roast marshmallows with no worries about what time to go to bed. That life was challenging, exciting and exhilarating in which you did not fumble and your words and actions were never hurtful but helpful to another. What if tomorrow's deadline was not crucial because there really is the next day, forever.

What if we were whole with no flaws, no pain, no sadness, and what if the only reason you cried was because you were happy?

Can you honestly look at the face of a small child and not wonder who created you?

Stop for a moment. Imagine that it is early morning, wake up and listen. Do you hear the birds whispering in the trees, greeting us each morning? Do you see the meadows filled with dragonflies and wildflowers? And who painted that landscape tucked back in the mountains with such intricate detail yet so simple and artistic?

Did you know you do not have to align yourself with a particular religion, but that you might, just seek a glimpse of the source of all that is?

I cannot give you any physical objects or material evidence to sustain my claim of such a place, only that I know that it exists and I hope you too have found Eternity in my journey, one that was not chosen.

Many thanks, to the following people.
They have helped edit my writings, and encouraged
and guided me through this project.

John Smith
Marsha Smith
Lisa Hardwick
Sara Wiseman
Lynne Black
Janet Del Ponte
Calli Hardwick
Samantha Enochs
Laurie Johnson
Karin Holton

And

<u>Dennis Miller</u>

My love, my soul mate, my friend, for standing
with me and beside me through the most difficult
journey of our lives, for holding me up through all
the struggles as I found my path towards these
writings.

Front Cover Photography-Dennis Miller
Back Cover Photography-Nicole Miller Ver

Jared Christopher Miller

Jared Christopher Miller

Jared

• • • • • • • • • • • • • • •

Journal Entries

January 17, 1999
Jared asks himself why he cares what another person thinks of him. He said, "I do know why and that is because I wish to have a positive influence on anyone… Then he quotes the following pieces as his guess to why he thinks he cares about other peoples opinions}

If I can throw a single ray of light across the darkened
pathway of another;
If I can aid some soul to clearer sight of life and duty,
and thus bless my brother;
If I can wipe from any human cheek a tear,
I shall not of lived my life in vain while here.
        -anonymous

February 13, 1999
You know it's weird to think, there has never been two waves to hit the shores of the world that are the same, sorta like humans. Life is peculiar, all the different people you meet to help form who each individual is, and how each person you meet influences that

individual. I am unsure what my future holds but I know it's in your hand (God) and that thought is so very comforting. I know that the difficulties which I'm facing will eventually aid me to help another. You are love and you are in everything, everyone. Through your love and showing your love even the toughest of hearts will weep and cry for you. If it is your will, I will follow.

August 12, 1999
I do know that working with youth is in my future, I don't know how much but I will help to show them the love that God has shown me.

Jared C. Miller
Ministry to Children
Hope International University
Alley S.
1/23/03

Assignment 1:

My passion for ministry is like this camping stove. The fuel, bottled tightly, can't wait to be mixed with fresh air and be ignited by a spark, to give light for guidance and heat for warmth. Much of my passion for ministry is still bottled up and waiting for the time to be ignited into a flame so hot that there is nothing that stands in the way of heating everything around with the same spark of love, that ignited me.

In itself, this stove is no ordinary stove. Specifically, it is a backpacking stove, one that was specifically engineered to endure the harshest natural elements. The format of ministry which I feel most passionate about is camping ministry. Any ministry position I enter, I hope to have such a powerful and welcoming flame of love, as God had for me, that the people around can do nothing but be warmed and ignited into an amazing relationship with Christ. It is clear that my passion for doing ministry in this fashion sprouted when I accepted Christ at a camping retreat and having memory after memory of camping with my family while growing up.

After witnessing eyes, minds, hearts and souls become opened to the wonders and greatness of God through His wonderful creation; I have become aware of the immense power and usefulness of using God's creation, the wilderness. It's, serene ability to push people beyond any and everything they thought possible in life and better yet their relationship with God is unmatched in the daily civilized lives that we live in society.

I do not know the question or topic that was posed to Jared, just his response above.

Jared C. Miller
Ministry to Youth
Hope International University
Dorado
2.1.2004

My Call to Youth Ministry

Time and time again the question of a person being called to
one particular ministry is asked to be addressed.
Unfortunately, this question is often made into something
larger then it truly needs to be. The call to ministry is not set
apart for a few Christians, it is something that is beyond and
quite frankly larger and maybe a little less definable and
broader then the majority of people desire. First off my call to
ministry is the same as everyone else's, it's a call to follow
Jesus Christ wherever He takes me, to love people, to minister
to their physical, mental and spiritual needs, and share His
Gospel.

During the eighth grade I made a friend by the name of
Brandon. Not far into our friendship he invited me a youth
lock-in at his church. After persuading me that I would have a
great time I agreed to go. I came away from the evening with
a sprained ankle and contemplating if God and Jesus were real
and, if so, what they meant to me.

A few weeks later, I recall Brandon telling me there was more
to church, than just fun games and good food.

Come winter, I went to the churches youth camp for their winter retreat. It was at this retreat that my relationship with God became personal and real to me. I remember vividly an evening Bible study with my cabin that I came to the realization that God desired a personal relationship with me and it was at this time I accepted Jesus into my life and the seed to minister to others through the camping ministry was planted.

During high school I got involved in every possible activity in church. I became a peer leader with the youth group and even started directing the youth bell choir for middle school students. It was between my junior and senior year in high school that I first thought about going into ministry full time after graduating. During a mission trip I went on over the summer I was given the chance to help lead an evening session and present a message to the youth groups from my region. There were about 60 students. It was during this evening session that I remember gaining an enthusasium to pursue ministry. Unfortunately, because of a miss led relationship with one of the females in my youth group and the disastrous breakup which followed, church became harder to attend due to the rising tension between my ex-girlfriend and myself. I turned my focus to school and more specifically theater.

Theater became my escape from the disaster at church. As I began to focus my time on theater I was able to become my own person again. I continued to work on my relationship with God but I had put it on the back burner, trying to avoid the church itself at all cost. I fell in love with the theater and all of the aspects surrounding the production I was working on. The next thing I knew I was filling out an application for Portland State University, to study technical theater. I was convinced the PSU was where God was calling me, therefore I only sent out one application.

Prior to attending Portland State I was awarded one of two theater scholarships for the University. At this time, I thought receiving this scholarship was a confirmation to study theater. By the second quarter at PSU, I was undertaking projects previously only given to upper division or graduate students. Adding to this instant fame, I was with working a professional theater company as a stage manager. Throughout my freshman year I gained more and more leadership responsibility within the department and lost more and more of my humbleness, gaining more pride and an attitude that said, "I can do anything, I don't need any help." I lost site of the need to have support from other Christians. Unfortunately, the price of my instant success within the theater department and the subsequent results left me feeling lonely, deserted and lost without direction.

After completing my freshman year, I took a job with the youth camp that I had accepted Christ at and attended throughout junior and senior high. Throughout the summer I began to realize the situation I put myself into and I didn't like what I was seeing. By the end of the summer I was determined to maintain a "good Christian" life while studying theater at PSU but had the increasing desire to work within camping ministry full time, since I was able to continue many of my personal passions such as ministering to people, drama and outdoor adventure activities.

Come fall I went back to Portland State to continue my studies. During the first few months back, I was unable to determine why school was not enjoyable. Even though I was working my second professional theater job, I felt as nothing was going well. I began to see that the gift of leadership that I have was not being used to its fullest potential through theater. I needed something with more meaning and ability to effect people for God. Seeing the need to remove myself from the situation I returned to the camp and worked part time maintenance while continuing my study of theater for the winter quarter. After coming to understand that PSU was not where God wanted me anymore, I withdrew from classes and chose not to enroll spring quarter.

I look back and see that my decision to attend PSU was more out of my own desire then my desire to follow God. However, in spite of this I see that God used my time there to prepare me and make my understanding of people into a more rounded view then I would ever gotten had I not attended PSU.

Moving into fulltime site staff at Camp Arrah Wanna I began to learn more and more possible ministries God could call me into. I saw that camping ministry was one in which I would never grow tired of since it constantly changes, throws curve balls at you and gives you the chance to share God's message and creation in a place without the normal distractions in the cities. During the winter months my workload was considerably less then that of the previous summer months.

This allowed for the development of an incredible relationship with my boss/mentor and his family. Having a camp as my background and playground I was able to spend much of my time talking with God and seeking His plan for me in ministry. Once the summer session was coming to an end I made the decision to move off the camp and began to focus once again on completing school. However, in searching for a new school I took the time and I made sure that I was seeking God's will and not mine.

Through my time at Camp Arrah Wanna I learned that ministry is not a normal nine to five job with the weekends off. **Ministry is a life style not a job.** I am incredibly thankful for the experience of living in a full time ministry at Arrah Wanna. Through this time I came to realize the potential ministries God could call me to. When I think about ministry I am excited for the possibilities of growth that I will be presented with. As I said before, my call is to follow Jesus wherever He may take me. I see that camping ministry is where I will start my "professional" ministry career but I know that my service for God is and in no way limited to this one particular field of ministry. The options are endless in regards to where God can and will lead me to minister.

Each day I gain more enthusiasm for the ministry opportunities that God has placed in my life. Every direction I look I see the possibilities that wait. I can't even begin to talk about the excitement that I have as I dive into ministry. I am most excited to see the passion that I have for youth and the outdoors, develop into a fulltime ministry where I can share

God's creation with youth that have never been able to experience it first hand.

This assignment was written nineteen days before Jared's death.

Jared

Along the road stands a cross
A cross for a man with a gentle soul
A cross for where he died

His soul – His spirit touched many
And many more

He stood, along that road
Not too far from the site
On his way to meet the Lord
Our God, of all Creation

He knew it was time to go
Yet he had to stop
He needed a moment,
Just a moment

A
Moment
to tell his mother goodbye

Vickie Miller

20554578R00127

Made in the USA
Middletown, DE
31 May 2015